From Foster Care to College

A Guide for Teens

By Youth Communication

Edited by Autumn Spanne

True Stories by Teens

From Foster Care to College

EXECUTIVE EDITORS
Keith Hefner and Laura Longhine

CONTRIBUTING EDITORS
Rachel Blustain, Al Desetta, Kendra Hurley,
Nora McCarthy, Sean Chambers, Jennifer Chauhan,
Andrea Estepa, Virginia Vitzthum

LAYOUT & DESIGN
Efrain Reyes, Jr. and Jeff Faerber

PRODUCTION
Stephanie Liu

COVER ART
YC Art Dept.

For reprint information, please contact Youth Communication.

ISBN 978-1-935552-46-8

Second, Expanded Edition

Printed in the United States of America

Youth Communication ®
New York, New York
www.youthcomm.org

Catalog Item #CW13-1

Table of Contents

Contents

Using the Book

Introduction

By Te-Li Shu

When I was 9, college was all my mother could talk about. It was always, "When you go to college…" and, "What do you want to be when you grow up?" But as I got older, my mother's mental illness worsened and things changed. During my last months of high school I was placed in foster care with family members. Every day was a battle with my relatives. Life became overwhelming.

I was ready to drop out of school and forget college altogether; I didn't think I'd be accepted. When I told my social worker, he responded, "I'm very disappointed in you. Why set the bar so low?" Then I thought, "If I don't try, I'll always wonder what if." I decided to go for it.

During the college application process I moved into another foster home, this time with strangers. There was no support. I explained things to my college guidance counselor and finally received help. But I often felt like I was running in circles. There was so much back and forth with my paperwork, all the documents I needed to prove I was really in foster care. Then I found out I'd been waitlisted by my top choice school. I almost didn't get in because some paperwork wasn't forwarded to me when I changed foster homes!

Luckily, we got it all straightened out, and I just finished my first year at SUNY Stony Brook (a public university on Long Island). It wasn't easy, but I survived, and now I can't believe I ever thought that college wasn't for me. My whole life I was very isolated, but in college, I found a community of people through my classes and study groups.

Unfortunately, my experience isn't as common as it should be. One study by the Casey Foundation found that less than half of the former foster youth surveyed made it to college or vocational school, and only 2.7% of those 25 and older had earned a bachelor's degree. This makes me angry. Young people who age out of care experience high rates of homelessness and unemployment. That should tell you that we're the very people who need college the most. Why isn't more being done to help us get there, and stay there?

Applying to college, and succeeding once you get there, can be two enormous hurdles for students in care. In the following stories, foster teens like me write about how they managed to successfully focus on college in spite of many obstacles.

We've divided the book into four parts: The first, "Is College for Me?", deals with the decision about whether or not to go to college at all—a common question for teens who may feel unprepared, who may be the first in their families to attend college, and who lack strong family support. The second part, "Getting In," takes a close look at the college application process, guiding students step by step through each stage.

Of course, getting into college is only the beginning. Making it through college to graduation comes with its own set of academic, social, and financial challenges. In the third section, "Paying for It," we give practical advice about financial aid and show how to tackle some of the common money issues faced by college students in foster care. Finally, in "Succeeding in College," we offer stories that provide a roadmap for college survival and success. Interspersed throughout this section are easy-to-read tips from current college students who are in foster care.

We hope the stories, advice, and information here will help you feel more confident about your own path to college. Use this guide as a starting point for seeking more information and talking to school counselors, teachers, and friends.

PART 1:
IS COLLEGE FOR ME?

Skyler Kane Kraemer

Learning to Believe in Myself

By Ja'Nelle Earle

When I was 16 and pregnant with my son, I decided I wanted to go to college. I did not want to continue my family's cycle of being low income and struggling through life.

But I didn't know the first thing about college. I did not know the difference between community colleges and universities, how to apply, or where to get the money. In all the group home schools I attended, I never heard a teacher even mention the words "college" or "the future" in class. We learned about being in the army, and plenty of teachers encouraged us to get GEDs, but not to aim for higher education.

Even though I worried I hadn't gotten a good enough education and might not be smart enough for college, I told a staff member that I wanted to go and one day become a social worker or counselor.

"You would be an excellent social worker," she said. She had a degree in social work herself and told me I could do anything I wanted. After that, we talked more about me going to college. I began to think that maybe my dream could become reality. I decided my goal would be to attend a four-year university.

A few months after I had my son, I left the group home and went to live with a relative. I returned to public school, which was a total shock. I felt miles behind the rest of the 12th graders. I felt like a failure and feared my dream of going to college might never happen.

I became really close to my homeroom teacher at the school, Ms. P., who told me, "You are really smart. You should apply to our local four-year university. I know you can get in!" She had more faith in me than I had in myself.

I thought I would be better off at a community college where I could make up all the requirements I needed to be accepted to a four-year university. So I took an assessment test for my local community college and scored average in almost everything.

The college was so big and I felt lost in a world of people who seemed better and smarter than me.

I applied for scholarships, but didn't get any and couldn't understand why. Not getting any of the scholarships made me feel like I was right and Ms. P. was wrong: I wasn't good enough for college.

Near the end of the year, I was supposed to fill out a yellow "senior datasheet" to be considered for scholarships given out by the school. Because I believed I would never be chosen, I didn't bother to turn mine in.

The day that the school announced the scholarship winners, I went into Ms. P.'s classroom for 5th period to do my job as a teacher's assistant.

"Why didn't you turn in your senior datasheet?" Ms. P. demanded. "I nominated you for a scholarship and you were chosen, but since you didn't turn in your datasheet, they won't give you the scholarship!"

I was so disappointed in myself. I couldn't believe that someone had actually nominated me. Because I thought the worst, I got the worst. I wondered if maybe I should start believing in myself as other people had believed in me. Perhaps that's what it would take to make my dream of college become a reality.

My social worker suggested that I attend Independent Living Skills classes to get more information about college before I went that fall. I was very shy and I didn't want to be in a group with people I didn't know. I convinced myself that I knew everything I needed to know. If I didn't know something, I decided I would ask my sister since she was enrolled at the two-year college I was planning to attend.

I wondered if maybe I should start believing in myself as other people had believed in me.

I got nervous every time I set foot on that campus. The college was so big and I felt lost in a world of people who seemed better and smarter than me. When there was an orientation for new students I didn't attend because I was so afraid of going on campus.

I also had trouble registering because I couldn't understand how people would leave a one-hour class at 9 a.m. and make it to the next class starting at 10 a.m., so I registered for only one class. Later I took a big step and asked someone how the class timing worked. I found out that teachers let students out from classes 10 minutes before each hour so students could be on time to their next class.

My sister told me that another way to get help was through something called the Educational Opportunity Program (EOP), designed to support first-generation college students, low-income students, and students who needed remedial classes. I applied, but I didn't get a response.

I was very disappointed because EOP had counseling and

other benefits like book grants, workshops, and a special graduation ceremony. I was too shy to ask why they had not contacted me, but I told my sister about my problem. After she talked to one of the head counselors, I got a date and time for orientation and I received EOP services, which helped me.

My first day of school was so scary. I still felt I wasn't good enough for college and I wished I could be home, spending time with my son. Then I remembered that my 18th birthday would be here in less than two months, and there would be no more foster care money. I was going to have to start supporting myself.

With that in mind, I was brave and went to my first class, English.

After working hard in the English class for one semester I earned a "B." I was very proud.

The second semester I not only took a full load of classes, I also found a job. I went to a program that helps foster and former foster youth get jobs and my case manager helped me create a wonderful résumé. Soon I was the student worker for our county's Independent Living Skills program, working 20 hours a week.

As time went on, college and work became creative outlets for me, which made it easier to balance work, school, and being a mother. That same semester, I learned of two scholarships for former foster youth. Like the last time, I thought I would not be chosen, but this time, I did apply. To my surprise, I was awarded both scholarships.

Getting those scholarships finally made me feel like I belonged in college. Through those scholarships, I found the financial and emotional support I needed to continue attending college.

I still sometimes felt inferior to other students, but I went ahead and applied to a local four-year university.

In March, I received a letter from the university and ripped it open. I was accepted! I kept reading the letter over and over to make sure that I was reading it correctly. I was very excited. I had thought I wasn't good enough and that I could never get through college, but through persistence, I had finally reached one of my long-term goals.

Two months later, I got my associate's degree. I felt good. I felt like I could achieve anything I wanted.

Ja'Nelle graduated from college and works as a residential counselor at a group home in Pennsylvania. She is married and has four children.

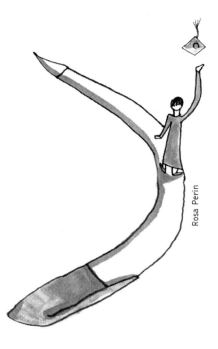

Rosa Perin

I Plan to Go to College— What About All the Other Foster Teens?

By Luis Reyes

I'll tell you something, every time I hung out with my boys Junior and Ray, college was not the topic we smoked. For a while, the streets helped me make my mark in the world without the benefit of a traditional education. I wanted to do something positive that would change my life around, but there was rarely anyone there to give me that kind of direction. Hanging out with my friends made me feel more secure and loved than I felt with my foster mom, my biological mom, my always-stepping-on-you step-mom, my adoptive mom, and everyone else in that system.

I never really wanted to get in trouble, but I figured it was the only way to get people to pay attention to the pain I was in.

I became a kid who refused to give a damn about anyone until someone gave a damn about me. I dropped out of high school at 16 and became an alcoholic, which brought me closer to my father but became a barrier to finding out who I was and who I could be. Seeing my own blood on the tip of my enemy's knife finally made me realize that the streets were not working.

After being out of school for about eight months, the decision to go back was not one I made in the blink of an eye. What helped me was my writing. I scribbled endless essays and poems on my sister's supply of construction paper, which I'd steal when she was sleeping. I wrote out so many thoughts but I had no one to listen to them. It took many nights of dreaming wonderful dreams of success for me to get up and say, "I want to succeed."

I became a kid who refused to give a damn about anyone until someone gave a damn about me.

When I went back to school, many people there noticed my talent for writing. That inspired me to keep working. I want to become a writer, a poetic mastermind. I want to travel across the four corners of life and blow words like the wind that will give strength and inspiration to those who need it.

First, of course, I have to finish school. I am now eight credits and two high school exams away from doing something that no one in my family has ever accomplished: receiving a high school diploma. And although it's taken me 5 1/2 years, it'll be worth it.

Once I receive my diploma, I'm hoping to get into Hosftra University in Long Island, New York, though I'm applying to other colleges, too. My dream is to work hard, improve my skills, and after four years, apply to Columbia University's Masters in Writing program. I yearn for the challenge.

I'm determined to make it, but I worry about the other guys in my residence. Right now I live in a type of transitional housing called Independence Inn. The program helps you get the skills you need to start walking the road toward independence. We all know that it takes more than a year to gain total independence, but that's all we have. There are 19 residents living at the Inn, including me. We all face the same issues: poverty and despair. But all of us also have strength in one form or another.

One thing I've noticed about the residents of the Inn is that most of them ask for the things they want right now, but they forget about what they'll need in a few months when they're on their own—like the knowledge and responsibility necessary to maintain their own apartment; a decent savings account in case they find themselves a little behind; a

Now that I see college as my next step, it hurts to see guys I live with give up on opportunities.

plan B along with a plan C; a résumé; self-esteem; a job. College is the last thing on most of their minds.

That's not true for all the residents. My boy Anthony already has his mind set on where he wants to go in life. I wouldn't be surprised to see him as my roommate in college. Then there's José. He is also trying to do good, going to school and holding down a job. His problem is that he spends all his cash rather than remembering to save. But he's getting there.

A lot of the other kids don't seem like they're going in any direction. There's one, whose name I won't mention, who's very bright and passed his GED with a high score. But he comes in almost every day under the influence of liquor or weed.

He'll lie all day on his bed, light-headed and dazed while the rest of the residents make fun of him. He seems trapped in his own little world. And every night he gets up and looks into the mirror like he's seeking some answers in his reflection, like he's trying to find his own self-image. He has nowhere to go, no job, and hardly comes to school. But he's scheduled to be discharged soon. He needs some serious help.

Then there's another boy whose name I'll also leave aside. He dresses in black, with black nails. I like to talk to him, but when

I do, I notice the anger he holds toward the world. He's another one about to be discharged. I fear for him, because he also has nowhere to go. He tells me, "I don't have a plan. I'm waiting for a plan to come to me."

Whose fault is it? There are so many answers to that question. Our parents, the system, our own—the fact that at 17, 18, 19, we live in what's basically a homeless shelter. For many of us, that's enough hard evidence to prove that life sucks and to make us want to give up.

Now that I've begun to pull my life together and see college as my next step, it hurts to see some of the guys I live with give up on opportunities they are blind to because of anger and hatred and despair. It's the kind of anger that chokes you until you suffocate, obscuring everything that's true.

College isn't the only answer, and it's not the answer for everyone. But the fact that it's not an option, or even a fantasy, for so many kids in care is a serious problem, one we all need to start addressing long before we reach college age.

_____

Luis was 18 when he wrote this story.

Stressed For Success

By Rana Sino

Have you ever thought of going to college? Lots of kids in foster care say, "No way!" Or when they hear the words "higher education," they just say, "Huh?"

Chris Bogle thought otherwise. Chris, a 23-year-old college junior from Brooklyn, New York, lived in a group home where a lot of the other kids would spend the day hanging out. Some were doing and selling drugs while Chris was in school, or just spending their days playing sports.

Chris said that when he told the kids he was planning to go to college, they said, "Yo, why you wasting your time with school when you could be on the corner making real money?"

But Chris felt like school could teach him about aspects of life he knew nothing about, and take him to better places than a life dealing on the corner. Chris also knew he eventually wanted to be a lawyer to make changes in a criminal justice system that he believes is "screwed up."

When Chris first came to the U.S. at age 5, he used to watch the TV show *Law and Order*. On it, he'd see blacks and Latinos getting harassed by cops, and people doing time for other people's crimes. That show gave him the dream of being a lawyer. Doing that, he knew, would mean going to college, and later, to law school.

Still, it took a while for Chris to get there. Chris's staff encouraged his studies, and he graduated from high school when he was 18 with plans to go on to college. But a few months later, he chose to leave the system and go back to his mother to give their rocky relationship another chance. Looking back, Chris wishes he had stayed on the independent living track instead.

"Even though our relationship was getting better, we still had problems," Chris said. "There were still issues between my sister and me, and my mother was always taking her side." So after about six months of living at home and working, Chris lost his patience and left again.

This time he enlisted in the U.S. Marine Corps. At first, Chris only joined the Marines

Chris felt like school could take him to better places than a life dealing on the corner.

to get out of the house, but he stayed for two years. In his teens, Chris had gotten used to group home life, where he'd been able to do just about anything he wanted. When he tried going back home, all of that freedom triggered more problems in his household. But in the Marines, Chris learned discipline. That, he said, was an excellent thing.

Eventually, though, Chris got tired of the Marines. There was too much brown-nosing, and it was too controlling, he said. But Chris knew the Marines would give him some money for college, so he researched colleges on the Internet and chose to attend Long Island University in Brooklyn. He paid for college with money from the Marines, and also from a state program called the Higher Education Opportunity Program, or HEOP, which gives financial aid and other support to promising low-income students.

During Chris's first semester in college, he met all types of people he'd never known before, like people who didn't believe in God, and people who were gay or lesbian. Interacting with them and making new friendships let him see a bigger world than he'd known in the group home. The classes he enjoyed the most were discussion classes in his areas of interest—political science and sociology (which is about why society works the way it does)—where he got to hear other people's thoughts about the world and share his own. All of that made him a more open person.

But during that first semester, Chris also found that all the people around him distracted him from his studies. He did not have to worry about his curfew, or teachers scolding him for being absent. With all this freedom, he got too caught up in hanging out, staying up all night playing cards and talking, or going out to clubs with his new friends. Then there was another problem: the beautiful ladies all around. Eventually, Chris saw that his grades were dropping, and decided that he needed to refocus.

Chris had been a good student in high school, so it wasn't too hard for him to get back on track, and once he did, he didn't find his classes too hard. In fact, sometimes he wished they were more challenging. If he could do it again, he said, he'd research colleges better and choose a bigger, more competitive school where he'd have had more choices of classes.

Still, life got hard for Chris during his junior year. Before then, Chris had a job on campus with flexible hours, but when he became a junior, he decided to work off-campus. Juggling the long and demanding hours in the office with his schoolwork was rough.

Because he hoped to be a lawyer, Chris found a job in the mail room of a law firm and eventually he was promoted to being a "very low level" paralegal, where he sorts and files and organizes lawyers' cases for them. It's not exactly a bounce-off-the-wall kind of job, but it does give him some experience in the field. That will make it easier for him to be hired at a higher level once he's in law school.

Like a lot of students nowadays, Chris also started to work because, even though his classes and books were paid for, he needed the money. And because he had left foster care, he didn't have any help with his room and board. (By his junior year, he'd moved into his own apartment.)

But working and going to school is stressful. Chris is stressed, in part, because being

Chris works all day, and then he jumps on the subway so that he can be on time for his evening classes.

a paralegal, especially in a high-powered law firm, is one of those jobs where you're always getting yelled at. "My bosses say, 'Do this, do that.' I don't have five or six hands, and I think, why are they stressing me like that?" Chris said.

He also no longer has the time to do all the hanging out that he was getting used to. Chris works all day, and then he jumps on the subway so that he can be on time for his evening classes, which start at 6 p.m. and end at 8:30 p.m. Sometimes Chris studies on the weekends or on the nights he doesn't have classes. Right now, he admits that because of his job, he gets by with as little studying as possible—something he doesn't recommend.

Although it's hard, Chris has stuck with it. He's proud of the fact that he's been able to hold his own at his job and deal with all the tension around him.

Chris's mother now brags to her friends and neighbors about her son being in college and on his way to law school. Some people won't even talk to their parents after rough childhoods in foster care, but Chris likes it when his mother brags about him.

"When people I've grown up with see me, they say, 'Wow, for real? You in the Marines? You in college?' I feel great every time

I hear my mother talk about me," Chris said. "For most people who come from a background and an environment like ours, college is not even considered. If you're even considering college, you should feel proud."

Rana was 18 when she wrote this story.

Lee Samuel

Can You Get to College With a GED?

By Samantha Flowers

Foster care can mess up your education in so many ways. It seemed like every time I got going, I had to switch schools. So, even though I got good grades and was always bound for college, I dropped out of high school to get my GED (a high school equivalency diploma).

I entered the system when I was 14 and in the 8th grade. I was getting C's and D's. I knew that if I wanted to go to college, I needed good grades, so I started studying a lot more and paying more attention in class. As the months passed, I went from being a D student to an A student. Nothing was going to hold me back.

I graduated junior high near the top of my class and got the highest scores on the state exams that year. When I started high school, I dipped my head into things that I didn't usually do to help me get into college. I joined the academic flagship club and honors classes. I was getting A+'s in all my classes and making new friends.

But meanwhile, the relationship in my foster home was becoming fragile. I decided in the fall semester of my sophomore year that I had to get out of my foster mother's home. I was happy to end up with Ms. Mollie, the best foster parent I ever had. But when I moved into Ms. Mollie's home, I had to switch schools in the middle of a school year.

I was a sophomore but had already been in honors classes and AP (advanced placement) classes. The guidance counselor at the new school told me only juniors and seniors could take AP classes, and that I'd have to "work my way back up" to honors classes. So here I was in history and English classes that I'd already taken in 9th grade, plus math classes I wasn't prepared for. I wasn't happy and it showed in my grades. I tried to make the best of things by getting to know the teachers and learning more about my surroundings. My grades gradually started improving. But then a bomb hit me: I had to switch foster homes again because of a stupid incident with one of the other kids in Ms. Mollie's house.

Even though I got good grades and was always bound for college, I dropped out of school to get my GED.

My new foster mom and I argued a lot and I had trouble staying focused in class. It was like I didn't see the point anymore. It got so bad that I just didn't want to do school. I felt like I was learning nothing, getting further away from college, and I was miserable.

One day I said to my foster mom, "I want to quit school and get my GED."

My foster mom thought it was a stupid idea. She and I argued for weeks about my decision, but I finally convinced her. Then I told my social worker, and she hated the plan too. She said a GED was not nearly as good as a high school diploma and that I couldn't get anywhere in life with a GED. But I had researched it and I was determined.

When my foster mom saw I wasn't going to change my mind, she helped me research GED preparation programs. This turned out to be a big hassle, because I was only 17 ½ and the rules said you had to be at least 19 or out of school for a year in order to take the GED exam.

I appealed to my old school to help me. The principal said I should just come back to school. I told them again that I wasn't being challenged in school and my mind was made up. The parent coordinator was the only one at the school who helped. She told me about a GED program called CUNY Prep that would let me take the GED sooner.

Because the program was under the CUNY (City University of New York) system, the students didn't have to wait until they were 19 to take the test. And the program teaches you more than just GED test prep. It also focuses on preparing students for college. Man, this sounded perfect. I passed the entrance exam and got in, and I was really happy. I felt as if I could finally move on with my life.

It's worth thinking it all through before you decide to get a GED instead of a high school diploma.

The first week of the three-month semester was all tests; they called it "Boot Camp." When I started there were about 250 students; by the end of that week there were 120.

The classes were great: I was actually learning again. The teachers taught us how to write essays and papers and gave us lots of projects. The projects were a big part of your grade. Throughout the class, you could take a test and move up to a higher level. I had to start at the beginner level of all the classes, but quickly got into one of the highest math classes.

I liked CUNY Prep and it prepared me very well for the GED test.

I had promised myself that I would study every day and get the highest score on the test. But I got distracted the day of the test and didn't do as well as I'd hoped. Don't let anything or anyone derail you before a big day of testing, is what I learned. Still, I had my GED and could finally move about in the world. At least that's what I thought.

I immediately hit problems because I didn't have a high school diploma. I would apply to jobs, and the minute they saw that I had a GED, all of a sudden they didn't need anyone to fill that position. And I mean jobs at Rite Aid and stores like that. Even online, where they don't know what you're about or what strengths you have, I've been told, many times, "Sorry, it doesn't seem you're qualified for this position."

OK, fine, jobs can be picky with their workers, but colleges shouldn't have any excuses. The U.S. Department of Education states that a GED is equivalent to a high school diploma in any state, so wouldn't that mean that you can get into any college, too?

But when I applied to New York University, a competitive private college, the admissions officer told me they don't admit students with GEDs. She said that I should get into a community college first, then apply to transfer to NYU.

I think it's preposterous that you're discriminated against because of a GED, as if that somehow makes you less hard-working or committed or smart. But I will not let all the rejections and people looking down on my GED get in my way.

I took some college prep classes at a community college, and after I got my GED, I took some more classes at CUNY Prep that I can use for college credit. I just took my SAT and I'm applying to a four-year college here in New York City. I also joined the City Year program through Americorps, a public service program, to get more leadership experience and money for college.

When things get rough in school, people think they can drop out and get a GED, like 1-2-3, and then they're done. But it's not that easy. You can get stuck on a merry-go-round of nothing, especially if you're under 19. And once you have the GED, there are more obstacles: jobs and schools that treat you like a dropout instead of like the accomplished and college-ready individual you are.

You can get past these obstacles if you work hard—I know I will—but it's still worth thinking it all through before you decide to get a GED instead of a high school diploma.

Samantha earned a full college scholarship and now attends CUNY's LaGuardia Community College.

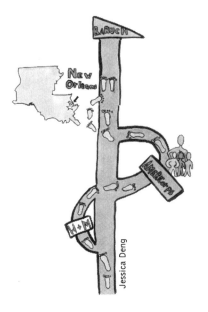

Jessica Deng

Delaying College Helped Me Grow

By Jarel Melendez

I was always big into education. I knew that's what would take me out of the foster care system and out of my surroundings, but I didn't think college was for me. I felt like I wouldn't fit in. I guess it had a lot to do with being in care. I worked really, really hard to keep up my grades in high school. Because it was such a struggle, I felt like college was above me, like I wouldn't measure up.

But my mentor pushed me to fill out college applications. He pushed me to do the SAT. I wouldn't have done it otherwise. I was intimidated.

I ended up graduating second in my high school class with a 3.6 grade point average. I was so proud of myself. Still, college was not on my mind. I had landed a job at H&M, the clothing store, and my job was my life. I was like, "Oh, I got H&M. I'm doing it!" I became a manager with H&M within a year, which is unheard of in the retail business, and you couldn't tell me nothing. But eventually I listened to people and applied to college a year later, in 2005.

I wanted to attend a historically black university. I applied to Xavier University, all the way in Louisiana. Xavier accepted me and I got some financial aid from them, but I had to get loans to pay for the rest. In August of 2005, I was about to go off to college when Hurricane Katrina struck and my university got flooded. So I went back to telling everybody, "I told you college ain't for me!" At that point, nobody could convince me. I was set. I wasn't going to college. I was staying at H&M.

I ended up graduating second in my class and I was so proud of myself. Still, college was not on my mind.

But then Baruch College here in New York called me up and said they were very inspired by the essay I'd written about my foster care experience. I don't know how my application traveled around to them. I think my mentor might have had something to do with that, too. He's been my mentor for years, and he's like a father to me.

I was offered full-paid tuition to attend Baruch. I thought, "OK, it's free. Why not? I'll go." But at the same time I had applied for an AmeriCorps program called City Year, because I wanted to devote a year of my life to community service. I was kind of sad because I didn't think that Baruch would let me postpone my acceptance and still keep my scholarship, but they did. Still, I had some lingering doubts about going to college.

AmeriCorps was so good for me. I really learned about myself. I worked in an elementary school for a whole year listening to kids and seeing them every day. I saw a lot of me in them. They would tell me, "I'm not going to college." The kids said they were unhappy in the projects, unhappy with their families. Just like my mentor had done with me, I told them that college would get them out of their surroundings. And then I was like, "Wait—I've got to practice what I'm preaching to these kids."

That's when I thought, "Baruch is a start." I graduated from the Americorps program last June and I'm about to start college. Wish me luck, because I'm also going to be working full time. I'm going to major in business marketing and minor in journalism. I'm so ready!

Thinking back, I wouldn't have been ready for Xavier in 2005. Even though I wanted to go far away from home, I would've been scared. It would have been my first time away from family, friends, and my mentor.

Joining the AmeriCorps program before I went to college helped me because I got to be around young people (ages 16 to 24) from really different backgrounds. Some already had a college degree, some had their GED, some were high school graduates, some were in the process of getting their college degrees. It opened my eyes and inspired me to want to get my degree, too.

Jarel attends Baruch College in New York City
and works as a youth advocate.

PART 2:
GETTING IN

Patricia Battles

Left in the Dark

By Shameka Vincent

It was mid-October of my senior year, and it was the first time I'd been called into my guidance counselor's office.

"Do you plan on going to college?" he asked.

"Of course!" I answered excitedly.

"Have you applied yet?" I was shocked that he thought I'd done it on my own. I replied "no," hoping he'd get the message that I needed help.

"Well, what are you waiting for? Applications are due around December."

"What…where do I go for this?" I asked.

"Just pick a school and go to their website and apply. If you need help, the college adviser's always available."

And that was it. The conversation I'd been waiting for since the first day of high school, over in five minutes.

"Just sign this before you go," he said, handing me a pink sheet. It was a letter of confirmation stating that he'd done his job and talked to me about college. Before I even left the room his face was buried in a pile of papers. I felt as if I was just another name on the list he could now cross out. He didn't even notice that I never signed on my way out.

I think that was when I started to give up on the college application process. Everyone I needed to help me was too busy. No one was serious about my future, and I thought that meant I didn't have to be, either.

For years, I had dreamed of attending an Ivy League university. I wanted to believe I was capable of so much, but I thought no one else felt the same. I was afraid of failure, of seeming vulnerable or weak. I was afraid of rejection.

So I threw the Columbia University application to the side (Columbia was my top choice school). Then, just a week before it was due, I started to panic and decided to fill it out after all.

With the chaos of going into foster care, no one seemed able to help me prepare for college.

When I finally looked closely at the application, I had to hold back the tears. Although my grades were decent, I had responses for less than half the things the application asked for. My school hadn't prepared me for this.

I was shocked to see that the application was so big on community service, asking for letters of recommendation from people other than high school teachers, and questioning the applicants about world events. Had I known, I would have gotten way more involved in community and school organizations, interned during high school for real businesses, and at least once in a while picked up the newspaper or watched the news for reasons other than my horoscope or the weather forecast.

I couldn't complete the application, so I felt that, as far as college and my future were concerned, I was screwed.

Although most of the application was blank, I still took it to my college adviser. Once she saw what school I was trying to apply to, she immediately turned me away. I was upset at the time, but now I understand why. Columbia is a school for the students who are prepared and serious about their education and future. How serious could I have been, coming to her a week before the deadline with a half-empty application?

My dream of attending an Ivy League college was what motivated me to work so hard in school, even when things were falling apart at home. Being accepted would show the world that I had made it in spite of all the obstacles. Now it was all over.

It wasn't until the college deadlines had passed that I realized it was my own self that had been holding me back.

I was upset, and I had to blame someone. I chose to blame my high school. What was the point of having guidance counselors and college advisers? The adults in my school had taught me very little about college and absolutely nothing about the application process.

Before the meeting with my counselor, the only information coming from my school about college was a few boring lectures from a handful of teachers and a once-in-a-blue-moon college assembly given by the college adviser. They didn't really think that was going to cut it, did they?

I needed to know exactly what colleges would be asking for and how to pace myself and stay on track so that I could provide them with what they wanted. No one ever broke all of that down for me.

Was I the only one who had been left in the dark? I decided to find out. I surveyed my classmates to see who had gotten help and why. The conclusions: Out of the 32 students in my AP (advanced placement) English class, only eight had guidance counselors or college advisers seek them out and assist them with the college application process throughout their entire four years of high school. All of them belonged to the honors program and five out of those eight had parents who spoke with these advisers regularly. The other 24 of us in the AP class, along with the students in my regular science class, were forced to fend for ourselves.

By April, it was way past the application deadlines and some of us still hadn't applied to college. One boy told me he didn't even know there was a deadline to apply to college. Get this: he thought you could apply whenever you wanted. Another girl didn't know that most colleges required taking the SAT or ACT.

The fact is, many students don't have anyone outside their school to turn to for help with college. In my case, my mom passed away when I was young and my dad abandoned the family soon after. Even if they'd been around, I'm not sure my parents even completed high school.

I had to admit that I hadn't made much of an effort to get the help I needed.

With the chaos of going into foster care, no one seemed able to help me prepare for college. My aunts and uncles all told me it was a must, but then just sent me back to the school to find out how. Once again in my life I felt abandoned. It made me not want to trust anyone and kept me from asking for help.

It wasn't until all the college deadlines had passed that I realized it was my own self that had been holding me back, too. I had to admit that I hadn't made much of an effort to get the help I needed. I asked myself: Is it the responsibility of the school to make sure we're fully aware of the college application process, or does the responsibility fall into the hands of the students ourselves?

Now I think that completing the college application should be a shared responsibility. It is the job of the college adviser to explain the process to every student. The school should make sure we all have a concrete plan for our life after high school, and help us make the transition. But it's also up to us.

If I could go back in time, I'd do it all differently. Freshman year, I'd immediately meet with my guidance counselor and college adviser just to let them know I was interested in college and start asking questions about the requirements. Maybe I'd join a sports team or school organization where I could build my leadership skills. I'd start watching the news and reading the newspaper. I'd research colleges and sign up for campus tours to start figuring out which college was right for me and what it takes to get there.

I'd decide on my top choices by the end of my junior year, and as soon as my senior year started I'd meet with my guidance counselor and the college adviser, who would already know me well because we would've been meeting regularly since freshman year. Together, we'd be filling in the blanks of the college applications.

---

*Shameka later enrolled at St. John's
University in Queens, New York.*

Terrence Taylor

Staying On Track During Senior Year

Are you a high school junior or senior planning to go to college? This calendar is going to help keep you on track with the application process. The clock begins now. Ready. Set. Go!

Before your senior year:

✓ Think about what you're looking for in a college: do you want a big school with lots going on, or a small school with lots of personal attention? Do you want to stay where you are or go to school far away? (See p. 70 for more ideas on questions to ask when choosing a college.)

✓ Meet with your guidance counselor to discuss your plans and ask questions.

✓ Start doing some research: check out the college guides at a bookstore or your local library, and look online. Some good websites to start with are The College Board (www.collegeboard.

com), CollegeView (www.collegeview.com), and The Princeton Review (www.princetonreview.com), where you can search for information on colleges throughout the country.

During senior year:

SEPTEMBER

✓ Continue researching colleges, and make a list of the schools you think you'd like to apply to.

✓ Visit any schools near you that you might be interested in.

✓ Make an appointment to see your college adviser. If you feel your adviser isn't giving you the help you need, make an appointment at a college access program, where a counselor can give you more attention. (To find one near you, go to www.collegeaccess.org).

✓ Register to take the ACT, SAT, or SAT Subject Test in October or November.

✓ Start working on your college essays if you haven't already.

TIP: If you want to visit a college, call the office of admissions before you go. All colleges offer tours and they usually have information sessions where they'll give you an overview of the school. Once you're there, walk around to get a feel for the campus and talk to some of the students.

OCTOBER

✓ Ask your teachers, coaches, and counselors for letters of recommendation.

✓ Take the ACT, SAT, or SAT Subject Test, or register to take them in December.

✓ Start looking for scholarships and grants (check out www.fastweb.com and www.scholarships.com, and talk to your caseworkers about what kind of scholarships are available through your foster care agency).

✓ Get started on your applications.

TIP: There are a lot of fraudulent companies that

run scholarship scams. Most places that charge you money for scholarship information tell you things you could have learned about for free.

NOVEMBER

✓ Ask a teacher, adviser, mentor, or friend with good editing skills to proofread your essays.

✓ Make sure that your recommenders have sent out your letters of recommendation to the colleges you're applying to.

✓ Here's another chance to register for the ACT, SAT, or SAT Subject Tests, or take them again if you're not satisfied with your scores.

✓ Apply for fee waivers to cover the cost of the application fees (most high schools give out fee waivers on a first-come-first-served basis).

TIP: Your school might not have enough waivers for everyone who qualifies. So if you don't get one, ask your counselor to write a letter to the college saying that you're a good applicant and requesting that they waive the application fee because of financial hardship. Most of the time, colleges will accept that. You can also ask your agency for help covering the cost.

DECEMBER

✓ Before the winter break, finish applying to all of the colleges you chose.

✓ Another chance to take the ACT, SAT, or SAT Subject Tests.

✓ Start looking at scholarship applications.

JANUARY

✓ Complete your Free Application for Federal Student Aid (FAFSA) form (www.fafsa.gov) along with any state aid applications. Go to www.collegegoalsundayusa.org to find a free financial aid workshop near you (or ask your school counselor or local college access program for help).

✓ Have your college adviser send mid-year grade reports to schools that require them.

FEBRUARY AND MARCH

✓ Contact the colleges you applied to and make sure they received all your application materials if you haven't heard from them already.

✓ Search and apply for more grants and scholarships.

APRIL

✓ You'll have received most of the colleges' responses by now, so consider everything there is to know about the college and make your decision.

✓ Tell the colleges you aren't going to attend that you've turned them down.

✓ Confirm acceptance with the college you do plan on attending.

TIP: If you've been in foster care and are under age 21, you can get up to $5,000 a year for college, through the ETV program. Go to www. statevoucher.org to see if your state participates in this program and to find out how to apply.

MAY

✓ If you take AP (advanced placement) exams, make sure the scores are sent to your college.

JUNE

✓ Have your counselor send your final transcript to your college. Ask them to give you an extra, *sealed* copy in case of emergency.

✓ Pat yourself on the back—you've made it through the college application process!

How I Overcame My Fear of Applying

By Debra Samuels

Let's face it—when it comes to applying to college, many youth in foster care are bound to be a bit nervous. I know that I was. You may feel that you're not smart enough to go, or you may want to go and don't know where or how to start.

Then there are those of us who start to apply and give up because we let the application process get us down. I had all of these fears but I overcame them, and you can too.

Now that I'll soon be entering my third year of college, I can look back at my senior year in high school and share some tips that might make the application process less frightening.

At the beginning of senior year when everyone was rushing to get their applications ready, I was...well, chilling! In the hustle and bustle of helping all the other students, my college counselor failed to realize that he had not seen me at all since the start of the year.

Soon, I realized how far behind I had fallen. At this point my counselor tried to give me a jumpstart by rushing me through the application process. During this time I wondered why it had taken me so long to get started. Then I finally realized the answer: I didn't think I could get into college, so I decided not to apply at all.

Most of the college-bound students in my school had extremely high grades and SAT scores. This led me to believe that unless my scores were as high as theirs, I probably wouldn't get into a decent school. That's a common mistake that students make when applying to college. It's especially true when stu-

I didn't think I could get into college, so I decided not to apply at all.

dents spend too much time comparing themselves to others. One thing that I learned is that everyone's situation is different and what works for someone else might not work for you.

Before I took the SAT, I was almost positive that I wouldn't do well. I didn't take one of the expensive preparatory courses that almost everybody in my high school took. Many people said if you didn't take a prep course, then you might as well not take the SAT at all. The counselors would even tell horror stories about past students who had done terribly on the SAT because they didn't take the prep classes. But when my SAT results came back, I was surprised to see that I had still done well.

Another thing that caused a constant uproar among the seniors was having to get recommendations from teachers. It's a hassle, because at the start of the school year many of your current teachers don't know you well enough to write a letter. This means hunting down teachers from past years who may not remember us well enough to write pleasant things. That can be especially hard if you've had to switch schools a lot because of foster care. (A word of advice: maintain good relationships with teachers through the years. When you're applying to college, you'll be glad you did!)

Thank goodness that I did some detective work and discovered that the letters weren't restricted to just teachers. Some schools asked for recommendations from just about anybody—friends of the family, adult acquaintances—as long as they knew you well and supported your application. So I used one from my music instructor and from the school counselor I was close to.

One thing that came to mind while choosing colleges was that I wanted to get as far away from home—New York City—as possible. Then again, I didn't want to go too far because our school warned us that everywhere was not like New York. Some colleges are in small towns that are not racially diverse or open-minded.

I think students who are in foster care sometimes have an extra worry when it comes to deciding whether to go away or stay. Many of us are afraid of losing our spaces in the group home or foster home if we go away for school.

I was lucky because when I came home from college on break, there was always an empty bed for me in my old group home. I always called my agency a few weeks before Christmas or summer vacation to make sure they knew I needed a place to stay. But not all agencies can do this, so it's important to talk about this with your caseworker before choosing to go away to school.

Once I took my SAT and decided to go away to college, I had to begin convincing the schools I liked that I was the student for them. If you don't do too well on your SAT and your grades are borderline, the student essay that most colleges require can give your application that extra push.

The essay is an opportunity to make yourself stand out from all the other applicants. You may not think there is anything interesting to write about yourself, but you'd be surprised. Anything that you do outside of your schoolwork is important to the colleges you are applying to. They are looking for well-rounded students, not bookworms or goof-offs.

If you feel stuck or are convinced that there is nothing interesting about you, then ask around. You'd be surprised at what some people know about you that you don't even know yourself.

Another thing that can help is describing anything that has had an impact on your life. If you are in foster care, I'm sure you have pages to write about that topic. It doesn't have to be a sob story, just a brief description of an event that altered your life in some way, and what you learned or discovered about yourself by going through it.

Maybe you want to talk about how being in foster care has made you determined to achieve as many goals as possible, despite the odds. That's something that I chose to write about and it worked for me.

When it comes to applying for financial aid, almost everyone runs into a few problems. One benefit that I had was that I didn't have to run around looking for my parents' tax forms to prove that I needed money for school. All it took were four simple words, "ward of the court," to describe my financial situation.

The sooner you start the process, the less complicated it will seem.

Another important thing to remember when applying for financial aid is to have someone help you. The whole process can be confusing and very frustrating at times if you try to do it alone like I did. Well, I learned my lesson and rushed to my college mentor for help after the forms came back from the colleges for the third time because I had left out information. After all the mistakes I made the first few times, I really needed help.

If there isn't anyone at your school who can help you, there are many other places where you can go for free college counseling, such as libraries, community centers, and even your agency. All you have to do is ask around and find them, because they won't come to you. And don't give up if you hit a dead end the first time or two!

Looking back, I just wish I had started the whole process a bit sooner so I could take my time with some of the decisions I made. The sooner you start the process, the less complicated it will seem. Even if you're just a freshman in high school, it doesn't hurt to begin looking around and deciding what you want to do.

Maintain good relationships with teachers through the years. When you're applying to college, you'll be glad you did!

On the other hand, it's really never too late to begin applying to school. Just make up your mind that, starting from this point on, you're going to try your best to achieve what you've already set your mind to do.

Debra was 19 when she wrote this story.

Leo Maisouradze

Bookin' It for the SAT

By Hattie Rice

Over the summer, I decided that I was going to study a little bit every week for the SAT. I was thinking about my long-term goal, which is to attend a competitive four-year college. I figured out a **coherent** plan and did some calculations. To master the most frequently used words on the SAT by December, I'd have to learn 250 words in 228 days. Maybe you're thinking, "Damn, that's a lot of words," but I'd be damned if all my traveling from my group home in the Bronx to the library in Queens (I don't like the loud libraries in the Bronx) was going to be wasted.

My goal is to get a score halfway between the average scores for Harvard and UCLA (University of California, Los Angeles). Perhaps you're thinking, "You talk a good one, but how you plan on doing that?" Well, the answer is very simple: by studying my trusty Princeton Review for the SAT—the next best thing to cheating.

The book is **didactic**, telling you the do's and don'ts of choosing an answer. (Thank the Lord, the SAT is mostly multiple choice.) The book has sections on the math techniques used on the test, the 250 most common SAT vocabulary words, and three practice tests so you can get a sense of how to take the test and what your real score might be. Sounds simple, right?

My first week, I found studying kind of hard because SAT words are so boring. I defined each word, wrote it three times, and used it in a sentence. I also spent a couple of minutes looking at the math techniques. Yup, extremely borringo. (Like my Spanglish?)

But I kept studying, because I knew that getting a good SAT score would be an **investment** in my future. I needed these words to succeed in college and to communicate in the corporate world.

The hardest part of studying is being mentally ready to do it. You have to make studying a priority even when you don't feel like it. A few bad situations gave me the **impetus** and drive to stay focused. First, I was often called "retarded" and "slow" by students and teachers when I was little, because I did not participate in class. I dropped out of school for most of a year, partly because I hated school and partly because I felt I needed to take care of my mom, who has mental health problems.

I set a goal of using at least one SAT word in conversation every day.

When I came into foster care a few years ago, I found that I'm actually good at school. (I have a 90 average this semester!) Now my grades **substantiate** that I'm **incontrovertibly** smart. The kids who still think I'm not that bright will think twice when I get into the college of my dreams.

Another bad situation is my group home, where it's more popular to chill in the streets than keep your nose in the books. Luckily, the more **contemptuous** I feel toward the girls in my group home, the better my study habits. Feeling like an outcast fuels me to study. Studying is my personal **vendetta**—I will show these people that the tension and negative energy in the house will not hold me back. I deal with my rage by pushing myself to meet my goals.

The greatest barrier to studying is that it's hard to concentrate when you have painful, pressing matters on your mind. My family is dealing with serious problems. My mother suddenly doesn't recognize anyone in the family. My father lost his job and my parents got evicted from their apartment. I'm worried about them, but I tell myself, "There's nothing you can do."

I hope that by achieving a good SAT score I'll be one step closer to graduating from college, earning a high salary, living on my own, and providing my mother and father with the help they need. I can only hope my plan will run **fluidly** because I'm very systematic and have basically planned my whole life. Plus, I'm very strong-minded (that's my way of saying stubborn). The only support I feel I need is from my bra.

To keep myself on task throughout the summer, I made sure I completed my SAT studying before doing anything fun. I also set a goal of using at least one SAT word in conversation every day.

After two months, I decided to take a practice test. I've never felt so remedial as when I saw the results. Expanding my vocabulary and thinking beyond the box are two of my finest qualities, but this test made me feel like a jackass. I got maybe three out of 10 right. My score **petrified** me. It seemed that I might fail in my quest to attend a good college and that I had studied all those hard words for nothing.

For a few days, my practice test score left me shaken. I felt scared of failing and suddenly doubted my intelligence. I wondered whether I would ever be ready for the SAT. What if my best was not enough? What if I couldn't achieve my goal?

Then I changed my perspective. I realized my score was just an indication that I could not be **lenient** with myself. I would have to commit myself to the task of learning these words, even though doing so will consume a lot of my time. I have to view myself as a wounded soldier fighting for her pride.

No matter what my score is, my biggest accomplishment may be that I've made myself follow rules even when I don't like what I have to do. I think it's great that I have so much discipline. It's a triumph that I've tried my best to excel no matter what **disconcerting** situations stand in my way. I hope I've set a **precedent** for my future. Living right next door to the projects and going to one of the most dangerous schools in New York City, I'm constantly reminded of what my future might look like if I don't go to college to escape.

> *No matter how well I do on the SAT, my score will be better than it would've been without studying.*

Ultimately, while reaching my goal has been more difficult than I had imagined, studying has been **salutary**. When I returned to school in the fall, I used my SAT words in essays and used my study skills to prepare for tests, and my grades improved.

I know studying will help me way more than chilling on the streets. No matter how well I do on the SAT, my score will be better than it would've been without studying. My goal will be tough to reach, but I believe in reaching for the moon. If I miss, I'll be among the stars.

Hattie was 17 when she wrote this story. She graduated from high school and went to college in upstate New York.

Improve Your SAT Vocabulary

Did you notice the SAT words in Hattie's story?
Here's what they mean — happy studying!

Coherent: Logically connected, makes sense

Didactic: Instructive

Investment: A contribution you make in hopes of a big return

Impetus: A motivating force or impulse

Substantiate: Verify something with proof

Incontrovertibly: Indisputable, definitely

Contemptuous: Scornful

Vendetta: A long feud or fight to get back at someone

Fluidly: Easily flowing

Petrified: Extremely scared

Lenient: Easy on, tolerant

Disconcerting: Upsetting, surprising

Precedent: A previous situation you can use as a guide

Salutary: Beneficial

Marcus Pierno

How to Write a College Essay

By Esther Rajavelu

Imagine sitting at your table and wondering what to write about yourself to impress someone you've never even met. Add to that the stress of feeling like the rest of your life may depend on what you write. For many people, that's what the experience of writing an essay for their college applications is like.

Personal essays are a required part of applications for most private colleges, and some public colleges. Some schools give you a specific question to answer while others tell you to write about anything you want. But all of them want you to use the essay to tell them something about yourself that they won't find anywhere else on your application.

"The important thing to keep in mind is that the most difficult task an admissions officer has is looking at a folder full of papers and trying to figure out who is behind the papers. That's where the essay comes in," said Ed Custard, a former college admissions officer and author of *The Big Book of Colleges.*

Helena Ku, a college and employment counselor, agreed. "They've seen the numbers—your grade point average, SAT— and they want to get to know the person behind the numbers, what you think and feel," she said.

For Jennifer Fondiller, a college admissions director, the essay serves two main purposes. "One is to see the ideas and thoughts that you have. Your personal background and upbringing and also the thoughts you have about the world around you," she said. "The other is to see your writing ability."

How important a factor the essay is in determining whether or not you're accepted "varies from college to college," Fondiller said. (It's "very important" at her college, she said.) As a general rule, community colleges and many state colleges do not require essays. But a really good essay can tip the scales in your favor at a selective college if you're on the borderline, according to Custard. If your grades aren't high enough, the essay gives you a chance to highlight other things you have going for you—personal qualities or special talents. And, Custard added, "strong writing always has a positive effect."

Fondiller agreed. "I do see students who write well, but don't do well in school," she said. "We then look at the teacher's recommendations, etc."

For many students, the hardest part of the essay is deciding what to write about. That's why Fondiller's advice is to start thinking about it as early as possible, especially if you plan to apply to competitive schools. "The summer of your junior year is a good time to start. It might take you three months to figure out a topic," she said.

Ku agreed. "Give yourself enough time to think about what you want to write because that process might take longer than the actual writing," she said.

If you think the way to impress admissions officers is by

writing about an "important" topic like nuclear energy or world peace, you're wrong. Write "what you feel comfortable writing about," said Ku. "Not what you think the admissions officer wants to hear, but what you want to write."

Everyone I interviewed agreed that it's best to write about your own life. "I would encourage everyone to write a personal essay," Custard said. "Why would you choose to give up the opportunity to show the admissions officers why you are an attractive student?"

If your grades aren't high enough, the essay gives you a chance to highlight other things you have going for you.

Fondiller agreed. "You shouldn't pick something you are not personally connected with or an entirely new topic to you. Just pick a slice of your life," she said.

For example, Fondiller said that when she was applying to colleges, "I lived in a town that was far from my high school, and I had a long commute. I wrote my essay on everything I thought about every day on my way, the people I met and how it really shaped my life," she said.

You should write about something that will "make you stand out in the crowd," as Ku put it. That's why Custard thinks it's best to avoid topics like "How My Coach Changed My Life" or "My Trip to Spain." "They are too common," he said.

Writing about a negative experience can work if it had a positive effect on you in the long run. "What you want to focus on [with negative topics] are the lessons you've learned and how that experience affected you or might affect you in the future," Fondiller said.

Even though the main purpose of the essay is to help the admissions officers get to know you, they also look at how well you write. "If it's good ideas without good organization, then it's not as attractive," Fondiller said.

It's also important to get feedback on the content of your essay. It's not cheating to show it to a family member or a teacher to see what they think. But remember that you're supposed to write about something that's important to you, not something that's important to your mother. "Consider the [feedback] of the source, but ultimately be true to yourself," Custard said.

When you're done, have someone proofread the final version to make sure there are no spelling or grammar mistakes. You don't want something as small as a spelling or grammar error to affect your chances of getting in. But don't give the essay to your reader the day before the application is due. They'll need time to do a thoughtful and thorough read, and you'll need time to make changes.

And, although it may seem as if your whole future depends on it, you'll write a better essay if you relax a little. "Don't make the writing an ordeal," Custard said. Fondiller agreed. "Just write from your heart," she said.

Esther went on to attend Wesleyan University and the Wharton School of Business.

Jessica Deng

Four Easy Steps to a Pre-College Plan

Jaleesa Suell went into foster care when she was 8 years old. That same year, she decided that she wanted to go to college. Over the years, Jaleesa worked hard. But the public school system in Oakland, California, where she grew up, didn't have a lot of college prep classes or other resources to help her get ready.

Now 18, Suell has come a long way. She just aged out of foster care and is about to start her freshman year at George Washington University in Washington, D.C., with a financial aid package that's paying almost all of her college expenses.

How did she do it? Suell was a good student, but she also got a lot of help putting together a pre-college plan. First she reached out to her mentor and people in her high school. Eventually, she got connected with a program called College Works, which helps underprivileged students get into private colleges—and helps them find the money to stay there until they earn their degree.

For many teens in foster care, college can feel like a giant question mark, especially if you don't have college graduates among your friends and family who can give you advice. That can be intimidating, and too often students don't apply to college at all. But it doesn't have to be that way.

"There's support out there, you just gotta go look for it," says Suell. "You definitely have to speak up and take advantage of it."

Here are some tips for how to get the college ball rolling.

1. Let people know that your goal is to go to college.

Reach out to as many people and organizations as you can for help as soon as you're thinking about college, so that you'll have a strong support system. Although it can be hard to get attention from a busy school counselor, principal, or teacher, it's often best to begin right at your school, says Kim Kiely, executive director of the National College Access Network (NCAN). From there you can investigate on your own and go back to them with questions.

Of course, it can be hard to develop strong relationships with school staff if you have to switch schools because of a change in foster care placement. Obstacles can pile up—transferring schools sometimes leads to academic setbacks and self-doubt. Afraid of being told that college isn't for them, students hesitate to approach counselors and teachers at their new schools.

Actually, says Kiely, that's all the more reason to speak up. Telling people about your goals and challenges will help keep you from falling through the cracks. Even if your grades aren't the best, letting people know that you're interested in college is important.

"Tell people your goals on Day One, then repeat it on Day Two and every day after that," she says. "Every time you change schools, tell your new counselors and teachers, 'I'm here now, and I've been on a rough track, but I want to go to college.'"

Do the same thing with your case manager, social worker, and lawyer, who can help you with financial aid opportunities that are just for students in foster care. And don't overlook people in the community, like mentors, friends, religious leaders, and employers. Take advantage of volunteer opportunities and internships where you can meet college graduates, and then ask them for advice.

2. Learn about college access programs.

There are more and more college access programs across the country like College Works, the program that helped Jaleesa Suell. Some work with you on the application process, while others, known as bridge programs, actually enroll students in classes on college campuses to give them a sense of what college courses are really like.

Even if your grades aren't the best, letting people know that you're interested in college is important.

TRIO is one of the biggest and most well-known of these bridge programs. It's actually made up of several national programs funded by the federal government to help low-income middle school, high school, and college students succeed in higher education.

There are two TRIO programs at the high school level. The Upward Bound program usually recruits 9th and 10th graders to attend classes on college campuses during weekends and summers so that they will be prepared for university-level work. It also provides financial and personal counseling, tutoring, mentoring programs and help with admissions and financial aid applications.

Talent Search offers most of the same services as Upward Bound, except that students don't usually take classes on college campuses. However, the program often has free tours and often overnight stays in dorms at local colleges.

The drawback is that not every high school has a TRIO program. But even if you don't have one in your school or community, you can still contact one that's nearby. TRIO staff may point you in the direction of help if you give them a call, and they'll give you advice on how to start taking charge of your own plans without having to wait for an adult to give you that first push.

3. Pound the campus pavement.

You don't have to be part of a college access or bridge program to get onto a college campus. If you're not eligible, or if you can't find a good program in your area, visit a local college on your own.

One of the best ways to find out what college is really like is to get on campus—any college campus—and start asking questions of students and admissions staff.

"Colleges don't have fences around them. So if there's a college in your city or nearby, there's usually wide open access," said MorraLee Holzapfel, director of outreach for NCAN. "Walk around and see what it's like, notice that the people are just like you."

To make even more of your visit, call ahead and tell the admissions office that you want to join a campus tour. Staff will often meet with you during your visit and may even be able to arrange for you to sit in on a class. After that, head to the library and stop by the student union, where you can grab a burger and start asking people what it's like to be a student there.

Although it's best to start planning for college as early as possible, it's also never too late.

4. Put yourself out there.

OK, if you're walking around a college campus, you're already getting out there. But there are plenty of other ways to find out about campus life and what it takes to get to college.

Start visiting university websites, where you can find out about everything from dorms and dining halls to admissions requirements and majors. Most websites have an online information form. If you fill in your address, universities will send out brochures and news about upcoming events and application deadlines.

When your high school has a college fair, visit every table. Ask lots of questions and get contact information from the college representatives so that you'll have someone to call when you have questions or need a helping hand.

Holzapfel suggests being open with college reps about your foster care experiences and goals. "Don't be afraid to tell people 'This is who I am, this is what I've been through, and I'm showing you the initiative and being proactive,'" she says. "That person across the table is going to recognize that, and you're going to have someone on your side when you're ready to take the next step."

Finally, although it's best to start planning for college as early as possible, it's also never too late. Whether you get started during your freshman year, senior year or even as a young adult, don't be afraid to take your future into your own hands.

Helpful College Websites

National College Access Network
www.collegeaccess.org
To find a college access program near you, click on the "National College Access Program Directory," under the Resources button on their homepage. You can locate programs by typing in your zip code.

College Board
www.collegeboard.com
This site has tons of information on college planning/preparation, financial aid, and college success.

Go College
www.gocollege.com
Click on the College Survival section. It covers grades, college social life, money management, health, and more.

Know How 2 Go
www.knowhow2go.org
This site breaks down the college preparation process by grade level for high school students.

Questions Every College-Bound Student Should Ask

By Latonya M. Pogue

These are some basic questions you'll probably want to ask about the colleges you're considering. You'll find the answers to some of these questions on the college's website, so check that first. Then, try to talk with current students as well as admissions officers or alumni representatives to answer your remaining questions.

☑ How many students are enrolled at your university?

Small (under 2,000 students), medium (2,000 to 10,000) and large (more than 10,000) schools can feel very different.

☑ What is the average SAT score and grade point average of admitted students?

Like it or not, you can get a pretty good idea of your chances for admission just by comparing your scores and grades to those who got in. If your scores are in the bottom quarter (or lower) your chances are not good, unless you bring a special quality or skill that the school wants.

☑ How do I apply for financial aid?

There are some basic things you have to do for every school, like complete the FAFSA. But after that, every school and scholarship is different. The more you know, the better your chances of getting aid.

☑ **What does the school cost?**

Every school lists its costs, but you must be sure to include every cost that will apply to you, including tuition, housing, food, books, fees, a computer, entertainment, and travel back and forth. The "hidden costs" can be larger than you think, especially when a single textbook can cost $100.

☑ **What is the average class size? Will most of my classes be in a large lecture format?**

Unless you go to a small college, you will likely have some large lecture classes—from 50 to 500 students. If you simply cannot function in classes like that, you need to look carefully at small (probably private) colleges.

☑ **What percentage of classes are taught by teaching assistants as opposed to professors?**

Colleges try to save money by having graduate students and part-time professors (called adjuncts) teach many classes. They can be great teachers, but they won't have the same level of experience and depth of knowledge that a professor does. If you're going to be paying a lot of money for a private college, you should make sure that you'll be taught primarily by real professors.

☑ **What is the average number of courses a student carries per semester? What are the maximum and minimum number allowed?**

At most colleges you must take (and pass) four or five classes each semester for eight semesters to graduate on time. If you don't, it will cost you. If you fail a couple of classes and have to take another semester, you pay for it. If you drop a couple of classes, you could lose your financial aid. (On the other hand, if you're very organized and hard-working, you may be allowed to take extra classes and graduate up to a year early.)

☑ What are the most popular majors?

If your main interest is English, and the most popular major is engineering, you may feel out of place. (Or you may feel special... it depends on you and on the school.) But it does make a difference in terms of the kinds of classes you have to choose from and the quality of instruction.

☑ Do you accept AP (advanced placement) credit and, if so, what is the minimum score you must have on the AP exam to get credit?

If you're counting on getting college credit for your AP classes, you must know the school's policy.

☑ Are there opportunities to study abroad?

Most four-year college offer this. But programs vary. If this is important to you, you will want to get details: How many students participate? What countries do they go to? Can you transfer credits if you go to a program sponsored by a different school?

☑ Will I be guaranteed on-campus housing for all four years?

It can be reassuring to know that there's an on-campus housing guarantee, but it's not essential. If you need private housing in your senior year, for example, you'll find it.

☑ What academic, health, and other support services exist for students?

Colleges offer a wide range of support services nowadays, but there is a wide range of quality. The only way to really find out how good they are for someone like you is to ask around. If you think you'll need tutoring, talk to people who get it. If you occasionally suffer from depression, talk to someone at the counseling center about mental health services. In a crisis, these services can make the difference between dropping out and succeeding, so you want to know.

☑ **How many minority students attend your university and do you have any special programs or services for them?**

You can usually find out the number of minority students on the college website. But who are they? And what services does the school have for them? If you're a black teen from the inner city and you go to a historically black college where most of the students are from middle class and wealthier families, the fact that they're black may not be that helpful, for example. One of the most important facts you want to discover is the percentage of people like you (e.g., black males) who graduate in four years. If that number is high, the school is probably providing good support. If it's not, watch out.

☑ **What kinds of extra-curricular activities do you have?**

Colleges often offer a huge range of extra-curricular activities. You're bound to find something you like, unless you have a very specific interest, like fencing. If that's the case, make sure the school has it.

☑ **Does social life revolve around the Greek system (fraternities and sororities)?**

If it does, and you don't plan to join one, you might want to talk to some students about what the social life is like for non-Greeks.

☑ **What does the area surrounding the university have to offer in terms of activities/social life/volunteer or work opportunities?**

There are a lot of great colleges in the middle of nowhere. If you want to volunteer in a soup kitchen, intern at a major corporation, or go to concerts and museums, it will be tougher in places like that. Look into what kinds of events happen on campus, and if the college sponsors trips to nearby cities.

☑ How big a problem is crime on campus?

Most colleges are very safe. You can ask about crime, or go online to read the student newspaper or the local paper to get a general idea of the kinds of crimes that get reported.

☑ Do you have ROTC (Reserve Officers Training Corps)?

ROTC can help pay for your education, in return for serving in the armed forces after you graduate. If you plan to enroll in ROTC, make sure your college offers it.

Thanks to Mike Mallory, former director of admissions at the University of Virginia in Charlottesville, for sharing most commonly-asked questions.

Karolina Zaniesienko

My College Fantasies

By Merli Desrosier

I have a fantasy of going to a fancy college, where college kids sit around having café lattes and cappuccinos and discussing what they liked about class that day. I imagine myself there—broke because it's an expensive school and I've just paid off my last semester's bill—but it's not that bad because one of my friends is rich and lets me be her parasite.

At the school of my dreams, I'm challenged physically, emotionally, and intellectually. I study all day and am with my boyfriend all night, because he tells me he doesn't see me enough. The good life comes with an expensive price tag, but it's worth it.

I've had this fantasy ever since I was little and watched "Saved by the Bell: The College Years." In college, the characters were still doing a lot of work but it was on a different level than high school. They could choose what they learned and the work was interesting.

After watching that TV show, even when I was having so many troubles with my father and with foster care, I was always sure that college would be the place where I'd find a better outlook on what life could be. Sometimes I'd cry thinking that there would be no way for me to get to my dream school. After all, where would I get $36,000 or more a year to pay for a private college? Not only am I poor, but I'm an immigrant, and don't yet have my green card.

Visiting the school made me think about the problems not just of getting in, but of fitting in.

I worry about my grades, too. While I'm a good student in some of my classes, and I'm on mock trial and moot court teams, not all my grades are great, especially in math and foreign language. I worry that good colleges may not think I'm as desirable as some other students. Still, I know that everyone who has gone on to a comfortable life didn't always have it comfortable, so I hold onto my dream.

That's why I recently went on a tour of Barnard College (part of Columbia University) in Manhattan. Barnard is one of those Ivy League schools that costs so much (more than $35,000 a year) and is really hard to get into. Only about 5% of the students at Barnard are African-American. I'm going to apply to other schools too, both public and private. But Barnard is the college I really want to attend.

Visiting the school made me think about the problems not just of getting in, but of fitting in. I felt intimidated before I even got to the campus. And once I was on campus, it was so big and beautiful, I felt like a scared cat in a big dog pound.

What struck me first was the fact that all the buildings on campus were well-constructed, made of either stone or brick, the kind of stuff you only see in rich neighborhoods where there aren't any guys smoking or drinking beer on the corner. The campus itself was absolutely gorgeous, with green grass and pretty green trees. I'm so used to being around buildings and concrete that it's easy to forget about flowers and trees.

I loved being there, but I felt like I didn't belong. The only people I could relate to were the people who were on the college tour with me. All of us seemed so amazed by all the college had to offer. It was hard to imagine being like the other people on campus, taking it for granted.

I think that if I do wind up at a fancy four-year college, it will certainly bring some conflicts. I'm not going to have all that I want, or as much as a lot of other students have, like support and money from their parents, or nice clothes and fancy holidays. I'm pretty sure that I'd change somehow, because going from being around people who have close to nothing to being around people who have a lot would change anyone.

But I don't believe that I'd reject anything that I really value in my life right now. I don't think I'd change my eating habits or drop all my friends. I don't think that if I graduated and became successful I'd necessarily even move out of my neighborhood (although I would of course get a nice apartment).

If you've had nothing and you work hard to have something, you're in a good position to help others as well as yourself.

There is nothing at all wrong with not being in the middle class and I'm not trying to run away from the people I've always known. I believe that if you've had nothing and you work hard to have something, then you're in a good position to help others as well as yourself.

And when I was on the campus, everyone I met was so nice, it surprised me. It also made me feel like maybe I could go to that school scared and shy, but leave it on my way to being a doctor, a Pulitzer Prize-winning writer or the next Martha Stewart.

Getting to experience a school like Barnard up close made me realize that lives like that are not only on TV. It made me want even more to have a life like that for myself.

Merli went on to graduate from Purchase College,
State University of New York.

PART 3:
PAYING FOR IT

Elizabeth Deegan

Where the Money's At

By James Davis

I always knew I wanted to go to college. Everyone in my family made such a big deal about it. It was like, "OK, you can get your high school diploma, but it doesn't stop there." Going on to get a college degree meant that I would have greater opportunities in the future. But I also knew my grandmother didn't have the money for me to go, and that there wasn't anyone else who was going to pay for it. So I figured I couldn't go.

At the time, I knew nothing about financial aid—student loans, scholarships, government grants, and other programs that help people pay for college. I'd been in the foster care system nearly 10 years, and in all that time no one had talked to me about how people without a lot of money pay for college. I wanted to talk to someone about it, but I didn't know who. And I never went to the college fair that came to my high school because I didn't see what the point would be. Why think about college if I couldn't pay for it?

So I just gave up all hope of getting a college education. I started making excuses, like saying that college life isn't for everybody. But deep down inside I didn't mean it. What I was hearing from friends, family, and teachers was that college is an experience that everyone should have an opportunity to try. I felt like a lost soul in the dark, thinking I would never set foot in a college classroom.

I came out of the dark when I got a new caseworker named Ms. Reese. I'd been out of high school for a year and a couple of months, and in foster care for nine years. I'd had so many caseworkers that I'd lost count. I had Ms. Reese for only a month and a half. Still, she changed my life. Throughout all the years I'd been in foster care and all the caseworkers I'd had, Ms. Reese was the first one to talk to me about college.

I'm trying to get all the financial support I can, because I don't want to have to take out any kind of student loans.

Ms. Reese told me about scholarships and financial aid—money that the government and individual schools give to help people attend college. She helped me complete college admission forms. She also informed me that in New York State, foster care will pay for your room and board up until your 21st birthday.

That was bad news for me. I would be turning 21 soon, and I wondered why I hadn't been informed about all this earlier. I think the first caseworker that I had in high school should've been the one to give me all this information when I was a freshman. If I'd had that information then, I might be graduating from college by now, instead of just thinking about starting. If it hadn't been for Ms. Reese, I don't think I would've gone to college at all.

After talking to Ms. Reese, I decided to apply to college. One day I started receiving acceptance letters back from the colleges. The first acceptance letter was from New York City

Technical College, which is part of the City University of New York (CUNY) system, and located right in New York City where I'm from. The following day I received another acceptance letter from Cobleskill University of Agriculture and Technology, which is a SUNY (State University of New York) school located in upstate New York.

I knew the two schools were very different, so I called Ms. Reese to tell her about my acceptance letters, and to see if she could help me make a decision about which college to choose. But I was told that Ms. Reese no longer worked there.

I want to become a social worker so I can inform students about things that I wasn't told, like how to pay for college.

I was hurt and upset. I'd hoped that I would at least get to share the good news with her, since she was the reason I'd gotten that far. But I wasn't shocked. I'd liked Ms. Reese, but learning she'd left was nothing new. I'd been tossed between caseworkers for quite a while. I knew having a good caseworker to help you see things through was too good to be true.

In the end, and on my own, I decided to choose the SUNY school because I'd heard so many good things about leaving where you're from to go to school. Now I'm 21 and in my freshman year of college. I like the college life but I still wish that I would've gotten here sooner, so I could have been with students my age.

And how am I paying for it? As of right now, foster care will only pay for room and board because I've already aged out (emancipated) from the system. I'm hoping that some adjustments can be made, considering my situation. But, in the meantime, I'm getting a lot of financial help from different sources, such as Pell grants (money from the federal government), financial aid that comes directly from my school, and money from EOP (Educational Opportunity Program). EOP is a program to help students who can't afford to pay for college.

I'm trying to get all the financial support I can, because I don't want to have to take out any kind of student loans. A student loan is a sum of money that a student borrows from a bank or the government to pay for a college education. But after that student graduates from college, he has to pay back the amount he borrowed with interest, in a certain number of payments.

A lot of people do take out loans and then start paying them back when they get jobs. But they face many consequences if they fail to make those payments every month. I'm not sure where I'll be working after college, so I'm trying to avoid loans, if possible.

I'm studying Child and Family Services now. My plan is to become a social worker so that I can inform students about things that I wasn't told, like how to pay for college. I don't want kids to go through the same things I went through.

If you want to go to college and you're in the same situation I was in, know that there is hope. Make sure you talk to your caseworker about college life so that you're not left in the dark. If you can't talk with your caseworker about your college plans, then talk to your parents, teachers, guidance counselors, or even your friends' parents. There's always someone out there who can help, if you're willing to speak up and ask for it.

James attended the State University of New York College of Agriculture and Technology at Cobleskill.

Maurice Anderson

Five Common Myths About Financial Aid

By Felisha Lewis

As a youth in foster care, you might be wondering how you're going to pay for college. There are many myths out there about financial aid that you might believe, but I'm here to tell you the truth. What I've learned is it's not as complicated as it seems.

Myth #1
If you're in foster care, you can't afford college.

Truth
Don't believe this for a second. There are many different kinds of financial aid available, and being in foster care usually entitles you to more financial aid and scholarships than you would otherwise qualify for. These include:

Grants: This is money given to students by the federal, state, or city government that does NOT have to be repaid. Most youth who have been in foster care qualify for Education and Training Vouchers, grants which give you up to $5,000 a year to use on tuition or school-related expenses (go to statevoucher.org for more information).

Scholarships: Scholarships also do NOT have to be repaid. Scholarships are usually awarded based on ability—for example, you may get a scholarship for having good grades or doing well in sports or showing leadership qualities. There are a number of scholarships created specifically for youth who have been in foster care. Make sure to talk to your agency and check resources like fastweb.com to see what you qualify for.

Federal Work Study: Students work on campus while they're in school to help pay for tuition and other expenses.

Loans: This is money from the federal government for tuition and other college-related expenses that MUST be repaid within a certain amount of time (usually 10 years) after graduation or leaving school. Be careful about how much money you take in loans, since you will have to pay it back.

Financial aid is not as complicated as it seems.

Your financial aid package will probably be a combination of loans, grants, scholarships, and work study. So even though you may receive a grant or scholarship, you will still most likely have to take out a loan. But it's worth it. Statistics show the higher your education, the more money you make later on. Paying for college is a smarter investment than wasting your money on unnecessary things like expensive clothes, jewelry, or a fancy car. The finer things in life will come in due time if you get your degree.

Myth #2
Applying for financial aid is too hard.

Truth

Of course it's hard. (Would you give your money away to people you don't know anything about?) It takes time. You have forms to fill out, deadlines to meet, and more forms to fill out. But you'll feel good in the long run when you get the financial assistance to go to college.

My advice: Get help from a school guidance counselor or other college counseling service. These counselors can help you fill out the necessary forms,

Statistics show the higher your education level, the more money you make later on.

like the FAFSA (Free Application for Federal Student Aid), state financial aid applications, and a college's own financial aid paperwork. Because forms usually ask for parents' financial info, they'll help you determine if you're independent or if a legal guardian has to include his/her financial background.

Myth #3

The only expense is tuition and that's all financial aid covers.

Truth

There are a whole bunch of expenses on top of tuition, like books, transportation, room and board, and activity fees (like I said, everybody wants money). Most grants and loans can be used for these college-related expenses although some are for tuition only.

Some foster care agencies will contribute to the cost of your room and board if you choose to go away to college and live in a dorm. Be sure to ask your agency about this.

Now, if you go away to an inexpensive college, you're much more likely to cover your expenses with grants and scholarships, so you may not have to take out a loan. You're more likely to have to take out loans if you go to a private school to cover the higher tuition costs.

Colleges also expect you to contribute in some way, either

through work study (working on the college campus) or by saving your money from your summer job. (But be careful—if you earn more than $9,000 a year, your financial aid may be reduced.)

Myth #4

You can apply for financial aid any time of year.

Truth

You can send in the FAFSA after January 1, to start school that fall. It's recommended that you do it in January or early February. (If you had a job last year, make sure to file your taxes as soon as possible, so you can include that information in your application.) In addition, each college has different deadlines for its own financial aid forms. To keep up with these deadlines, ask for financial aid information when you request the regular application. Scholarship applications vary, too, so keep a calendar with the deadlines of all the scholarships and other sources of aid that you intend to apply for.

Here's a little tip: Make photocopies of EVERYTHING you send to colleges, including applications and essays!

Myth #5

You have no one to help you.

Truth

There are a lot of people and places you can go to for help. If you have any questions, contact the financial aid office at the college you plan to attend, your high school guidance counselor, your foster care agency, or a college access or counseling program in your area (search for one at www.collegeaccess.org).

Felisha was 17 when she wrote this story.
She later graduated high school.

Jessica Deng

Financial Aid 101

To find out how former foster youth (and those who have aged out) can finance a college education, we broke it down with John Emerson, senior manager of education for Casey Family Programs in Seattle, Dorothy Ansell assistant director of the National Resource Center for Youth Services in Tulsa, Oklahoma, and Eileen McCaffrey, executive director of the Orphan Foundation of America in Virginia. Here's what they told us.

Q: Is there financial aid especially for students in foster care?

A: It may be possible for you to get a college degree without ever paying a dime—especially if you live in a state such as Texas, Maine, Kansas, West Virginia, or Oklahoma that provides foster care tuition waivers. These waivers allow you to attend any public college or university in that state for free.

Some scholarships and other sources of aid are especially for students in foster care. Two examples are Education and Training

Vouchers (ETV) and the Orphan Foundation of America/Casey Family scholars program.

Every student who has aged out of foster care or who has been adopted out of foster care after age 16 is eligible for an ETV until age 23. ETV's range up to $5,000 a year and can be used not only to pay for tuition, but for anything you need to stay in school (daycare, rent, books, and more).

There are two conditions to get an ETV: You must be enrolled in college or a vocational-technical school by age 21. Also, you have to be making OK grades. Grade requirements vary from state to state, but you usually have to earn a minimum of a 2.0 or 2.5 grade point average—at least a C. And you must apply before you turn 21.

If you're in foster care, it may be possible for you to get a college degree without ever paying a dime.

The Orphan Foundation of America/Casey Family Scholars program gives out grants of $1,500 to $10,000 a year to students under 25 who were in foster care for at least one year before their 18th birthday or high school graduation.

Q: What other kinds of aid might I be eligible for?

A: All low-income students can apply for federal Pell grants, state funds such as Tuition Assistance Programs, and a wide variety of private scholarships. Many private scholarships go unused because no one even bothers to apply. The college you choose to go to may also have its own scholarships and financial aid, so you should ask the financial aid officer at each college what's available when you apply.

Q: How do I get started applying for financial aid?

A: To get the best financial aid package, it's important that you start the application process early, earn good grades, and be aggressive about digging up scholarships. It's also important to find a financial aid coach to help you get the money you'll need for school.

Juniors in high school who know where they want to go should call the college or vocational program they want to attend and make an appointment with a financial aid counselor.

Also ask your social worker, independent living coordinator, and high school guidance counselor to help you figure out how you can finance college. Tell guidance counselors and college financial aid counselors that you will be aging out of foster care soon and will be on your own so they can target scholarships, grants, and other financial aid especially designed for you.

The procedures for getting your ETV and other grants specifically for youth aging out of the system vary from state to state. Ask your social worker or independent living program coordinator how to get this money. It's their job to know. Then, during the fall of your senior year, start filling out the FAFSA.

Q: I always hear people talking about that. What exactly is the FAFSA?

A: The FAFSA (Free Application for Federal Student Aid) determines whether you can get Pell grants, Federal Supplemental Educational Opportunity Grants, Federal Work Study and low-interest loans. That means it's a must. You can find it online at www.fafsa.ed.gov.

IMPORTANT: Make sure when you complete the FAFSA you answer "yes" to the question that asks if you were a ward or dependent of the court. Answering "yes" will make you eligible to receive more money. It's important to have your financial aid coach look over your FAFSA application before you submit it, just to make sure you haven't made any mistakes.

Q: Can I receive financial aid if I'm not a full-time student?

A: Yes, usually you can get some financial aid if you carry at least nine credits. (In most colleges, each class counts for three credits.) You can get an ETV of up to $2,500 a year if you're a part-time student. You can also get a Pell grant from the federal government for part-time enrollment. This is a good option if you want to get an education but don't feel you can handle a full-time course load.

Q: I'm afraid to take out a loan. What can I do?

A: Borrowing money to get a degree from an inexpensive public college is a good investment. It's OK to arrange a low-interest educational loan through your college financial aid counselor to borrow a few thousand dollars a year. Just make sure you really do get your degree or certificate!

It's actually a good idea to borrow money and invest in your future, as long as you borrow only what you need.

Think more carefully about borrowing tens of thousands of dollars to attend a private college. And beware of expensive private trade schools: borrowing money to attend these kinds of schools can put you deep in debt before you know it. As a general rule, never borrow money to attend a private trade school.

Also, ask your social worker or independent living coordinator if there are any other government scholarships besides the ETV you can apply for. Different states have different funds available, and there may be something for you.

Q: I was adopted out of foster care. Am I still eligible for help?

A: Yes. And since 2009, there's more help than before. In the past, most need-based government programs, such as Pell grants, took your adoptive parents' income into account when deciding the amount of your financial aid package—basically, the federal government expected your adoptive parents to help you pay for college. But that's no longer the case.

Now the federal government considers you an independent student and will only look at your income (if you have one)—not your parents'—which means you could get more financial aid. Make sure you still answer "yes" when asked if you were in foster care or a dependent of the court/ward of the state at age 13, even if you were adopted after that age. (Rules for state grants may be different, so ask your counselor about that.)

Q: If I want to become a hairdresser, mechanic, or dental assistant, am I still eligible for financial aid?

A: In most cases, yes—but again, you should be careful when you choose a vocational/technical trade school. Many of these programs are extremely misleading, so be very skeptical. Before you enroll in a school that gives you a credential to be a nurse, dental assistant, mechanic, radio D.J., or any other certificate, interview people who do hiring for the kind of job you hope to have. Ask them if the school you're interested in provides good training. If they say "no," ask which schools do and go to one of them instead.

You want to be confident that you can land a good job when you complete your training. Instead of a private trade school, consider a local community college or non-profit program that offers similar training.

You can get only one grant per school per year, so if you realize the school isn't any good and leave, you will lose time and waste money. When deciding on a school, look up their graduation and retention rates ("retention" means how many freshmen students return to school the following fall to continue their studies). You can find this at www.nces.ed.gov/collegenavigator. A school with a low graduation and retention rates (less than 50%) is not doing a good job at supporting its students—and that means you should probably consider a different choice.

Also, make sure the program you attend is eligible for ETV support because some schools and programs don't qualify. Your independent living worker or your state's ETV coordinator can help you find this out.

Financial Aid Resources

Orphan Foundation of America
www.orphan.org
At this website, you can apply for lots of different financial aid that is designated to help current and former foster youth, including Education and Training Vouchers and Casey Scholarships.

The Free Application for Federal Student Aid (FAFSA)
www.fafsa.ed.gov
The FAFSA is the first step to receiving any kind of federal aid and can be completed online at this site. The website lists FAFSA application deadlines state by state and answers basic questions you might have about your eligibility.

www.finaid.org
This amazing website gives tips on filling out your FAFSA, provides a guide to the very diverse world of private scholarships (including scholarships for "skateboard activists," left-handed people, and obese students). It also gives information on student loans and how to avoid scholarship scams, and has a special section for students interested in careers in the military.

www.nces.ed.gov/collegenavigator
Use the search bar on the left to look up schools you're interested in and get info on their tuition, financial aid, graduation rates, and more.

Karolina Zaniesienko

The College of My Dreams With No Money Down

By Lishoné Bowsky

When you're in care, people often say you can't go to the school of your choice because it's too expensive. While the price of your school is an important consideration, I'm here to tell you that you shouldn't automatically rule out schools with high price tags. There are scholarships available for everything under the sun, including scholarships for being in foster care. If you're willing to do some research, those scholarships may help you cover the high cost of college.

You probably already know about your basic federal financial aid. (If you need information, ask your social worker or school counselor about applying for it, and check out www.fafsa. gov.) Each state also offers its own financial aid.

But sometimes that money isn't enough. I attend New York

Institute of Technology. It's a privately-funded college (which means that the government doesn't run it), and the tuition is extremely high.

My state and federal financial aid covered about half of my tuition for this year, and I could have taken out loans to cover everything else. But if you're like me, you don't like owing people money. That's why I decided to get some scholarships.

I think the best place to start looking is to ask the colleges you're interested in what kind of scholarships they offer. Individual colleges often give out the biggest scholarships, and you often don't even have apply for them. But it's good to ask about them anyway, because each one is different and some schools have more scholarship money available than others.

My school gave me two academic scholarships: a transfer scholarship because I transferred from another school, as well as an academic scholarship based on my GPA, which was strong after my first two years in college.

Despite these scholarships and other financial aid, I was still going to owe money, so I decided to try to find other scholarships. I began by looking through scholarship books. Those are books that tell you about all sorts of organizations giving out college money for all sorts of reasons. You can find those books in the library, or search online resources like ScholarshipHelp.org.

Don't automatically rule out schools with high price tags. There are scholarships available for everything under the sun.

I encourage everyone to give it a try because you might just find the perfect scholarship for you. But to tell you the truth, I found those books confusing. After 10 minutes, I felt as if I was becoming cross-eyed, so I decided to ask around instead. It's a good idea to ask people in your agency, your mentors, your teachers, your guidance counselor, your lawyer, your boss, whoever you know, about scholarships. You never know who might know about one you can apply for.

I had a friend who knew about a scholarship called the Orphan Foundation of America (OFA) Scholarship. OFA is a non-profit organization whose mission is to provide opportunities for foster youth to continue their education and pursue their dreams.

I think the best place to start is to ask the colleges you're interested in what kind of scholarships they offer.

This scholarship was a lifesaver for me. I received $3,000. It kept me from having to take out a student loan. In fact, when I combined my financial aid with all my scholarships, I actually had a little money left over to put in the bank.

So don't think that just because you're in foster care, you can't attend an expensive private college. There are ways around the cost. You just have to search and make it happen. While I know it's a pain in the behind, it is well worth it in the end.

Lishoné was in college when she wrote this story.

Marc Mazurkiewicz

How a Green Card Helps You Pay for College

By Leana

It was the opportunity to go to college and the possibility of a better life that drove me to remain in the U.S. when my mother returned to the Caribbean. My mother thought she had left me in a safe, stable environment, but things quickly turned sour with my living arrangement in Brooklyn, New York.

That is how, at 17, I found myself at Covenant House, a shelter for homeless teens. The counselors called the city's child welfare agency and I soon became a foster child.

From the moment I was placed in care, my caseworker and I told my agency that I needed a green card, the document that allows non-U.S. citizens to remain in the United States as legal, permanent residents. New York State law says that foster care agencies must help foster children obtain all the resources and skills that will enable them to be independent adults. This includes helping them get driver's licenses, Social Security cards, and green cards.

It's important to get a green card because without one, you can't work or remain in the U.S. legally. Some foster children don't have legal permission to be in the U.S., but many undocumented foster children are eligible to get legal permanent resident status. And that's very important when it comes to paying for college.

Last March, when I went to apply to college at the State University of New York (SUNY) office, the admissions officer was very encouraging. He informed me that I had an excellent chance of getting into a good SUNY college, but because I could not afford to pay for college, I had to get my green card first so I could qualify for financial aid.

Because I couldn't afford college, I had to get my green card first so I could qualify for financial aid.

When I told him of my dilemma, he went out of his way to try to help me. On one occasion he even called my social worker, who assured him I would have my green card within a month.

I later discovered my social worker had not even begun the process. As precious time passed, the only response I got from my agency was to "be patient." I waited and waited and waited. Even after graduating high school, I waited. But without my green card, I was unable to get employment or to qualify for college financial aid.

My agency said it couldn't give me any financial support for college due to the latest budget cuts in the system. So for months my life was put on hold as I lived in unbearable and sometimes abusive foster homes when I should have been in a college dorm, studying and preparing to become a productive member of society.

As I neared my discharge date with my green card nowhere

in sight, my social worker was still not helping me. So I decided to take the initiative and seek help elsewhere. An adult referred me to The Door, a youth center in Manhattan. The Door finally gave me the legal help and advice that I needed (for free!). Their staff attorney helped me fill out the green card application forms. The process of filling out the application and getting a medical exam, photos, and fingerprints was well worth it.

With the help of Yvette (my new social worker) and the attorney, I was able to get help because I was persistent. Now I have an appointment to get a permit so I will be able to work here legally. Soon I'll get my green card and be on my way to college.

How To Get a Green Card

By Theresa Hughes
Child Advocacy Clinic, St. John's University

In general, it's hard for non-citizens to get legal status in the U.S. But there is a way for some undocumented youth in foster care to get green cards. It's called Special Immigrant Juvenile Status (SIJS).

If you answer "yes" to ALL of the following questions, then you may want to apply for SIJS. (Note: If you're not sure of the answer, be sure to talk with a lawyer who can help you find out if you have something like an "open case" mentioned in number 1.)

1. Do you have an open juvenile delinquency, abandonment, or child abuse/neglect case?
2. Is the plan for you to *not* get back together with your parents?
3. Will the court find that it is not in your best interest to be returned to your home country?
4. Are you under age 21?
5. Are you single (not married)?

If your SIJS application is granted, you will be entitled to live and work in the U.S. permanently and to travel in and out of the country as a permanent resident. After five years, you can apply for U.S. citizenship.

It costs money to apply for your green card, but your agency is supposed to pay for it.

If you want to learn more about SIJS or apply, tell your law guardian and your caseworker as soon as possible. If you couldn't answer "yes" to all of those questions but you are still under 21, you should still contact a lawyer to determine if you are eligible for SIJS or other immigration assistance.

Jessica Deng

There's Always a Choice

By Xavier Reyes

In high school I lived in a group home, and a lot of staff and counselors there had high hopes for me. I was in special education but I fought to get out.

I attended an alternative high school that had smaller classes. I really liked that. The teachers focused on me and really wanted to see me excel. I paid attention in class, and I knew how to use words well. My college counselor told me I needed to apply for scholarships. That was a big thing: having people at my back who encouraged me.

Back then, the things that worried me about college were my lack of money, doubts about whether I could handle it academically, and my own sense of stigma about being in foster care. Plus I was thinking about aging out of care and wondering what I was going to do. I didn't want to leave one system just to end up in another, like welfare.

I graduated salutatorian and I was accepted to Pace University in New York. I enrolled at Pace, but I wasn't ready for it. I soon dropped out. I'd received a renewable $1,000 scholarship from the United Federation of Teachers to attend Pace. After I dropped out, I lost that. I continued working, but I felt pressure from everyone—friends, family, mentors—to go back to college. So five years after I graduated from high school, I enrolled at a different college.

Foster care always gave me the message that I didn't have choices. The fact is, there's always a choice.

I was not making enough money, and every semester was a challenge. I resisted taking out loans. After a year I transferred to a community college. I hated it—it felt like high school. But I stuck it out for two semesters before I dropped out and went to work full-time.

At that point, I was definitely more concerned about my own livelihood than an education, because by then I was aging out of the system, and the comfort I had known with foster care was gone. So it was sort of pick and choose—do you want to be educated or do you want to survive? I wanted to survive. I needed to work and I needed a place to live. I needed to get myself together. School had to wait.

Eventually my home environment became more stable. I was living on my own and the bills were coming in, but I was in a much better mental state to handle school and the responsibilities that came with it. I applied to Baruch College and got a $20,000 scholarship. Baruch accepted about half the credits I'd earned already.

My scholarship paid for my tuition, but I had to pay for my own books and living expenses. Money was tight, and, because I was living independently, my choice was get a loan or drop out again. I didn't want to take out loans, but in the end I had to. Looking back, loans aren't really a bad thing. I've learned that an educational loan is really an investment in my own future.

I did my full four years at Baruch and finally graduated with a degree in Public Affairs. The whole time I worked full time and had a full class load.

Foster care always gave me the message that I didn't have choices. The fact is, there is always a choice. Today I sit on the committee that awarded me my scholarship to attend Baruch. I see a lot of applications that don't show much effort. You can tell that an adult just told the kid to fill out the application, but the kid didn't really try.

It's the same thing in foster care. A lot of times, no one sits down with the students and helps them with their essay, makes sure that it looks "college ready." No one's guiding them. Their responses on the applications are very generic.

I've learned that you have to distinguish yourself, especially if you want to get into a particular field or college and get scholarships. A little effort goes a long way. My advice would be to not wait for someone to show you the way when it comes to college. Ask and keep asking and put some time into figuring things out. It's not easy, but in the end it really is you who has to make the choice.

Xavier graduated from Baruch College. He went on to attend graduate school and works at a major media company.

PART 4:
SUCCEEDING IN COLLEGE

Skyler Kane Kraemer

Me vs. The World

By Joseph Alvarez

It was time to go. My stuff was all packed up in the back of the truck. My staff, Sue and Randy, were ready to pull away from my group home. But, damn, I didn't want to leave. "Why can't I stop looking at this old-ass house?" I thought.

Bill, one of the group home staff, was standing in the drive-way, and some kids were sticking their heads out the window. I felt like they were staring at a ghost.

I was usually the one giving "words of wisdom" to the other kids, telling them, "Never get used to this sh-t, the group home is not forever!" Now I found myself wanting to hold on to this place. Why was I feeling scared, abandoned, lonely?

"Joey," Bill said in a joking way, "Are you ready, man?"

I laughed and said, "Yeah…Yeah, I'm ready." Playfully pre-tending to punch me he said, "Knock 'em dead, man!" He gave me a hug and that was it. SLAM! I shut the car door and I was off to college. Life after the system had officially begun.

"Man, me going off to college? This can't be happening. Kids like me don't make it this far," I thought, feeling excitement and fear as we drove toward Manhattan. It was 45 minutes but felt like 40 days and 40 nights.

After eight long spiraling years in care, I was on my own with $3,000 I had saved up from my summer job. I felt rich and free and sure of myself. I knew I was going to make it.

When the car stopped, we were in front of my dorm at the School of Visual Arts in downtown Manhattan, where I was to study film editing. "Damn, this is an ugly building," I thought. The place looked worse than the group home! I checked in and began unpacking my stuff. As Randy handed me the last of my things, I knew it was me versus the world.

We parted ways with hugs and words of encouragement. Then it was just me, my stuff, and my feelings of uncertainty. I almost felt like the walls of the small room were closing in on me. Only God knew how scared I really was that day.

When I first came to the group home at 10 years old, I had hated myself, the people around me, and anybody who tried to help. I felt the world had already killed my parents and my grandma, and I was going to be the next to die.

For the next four years, I was a walking time bomb. Even if you didn't cross me you were going to get it! Why? Because fighting was my way of showing the world how helpless and hurt I felt inside. How else does a young boy cope when everything he ever loved gets snatched from his heart?

By the time I was 14, most of the staff and social workers had checked me off as a kid who would amount to nothing—except one staff. Hobin was one of the coolest guys you'll ever meet. He was also an ex-crackhead and former alcoholic, so let's just say he had a sixth sense for detecting somebody trying to get over.

One night I had returned to the house real late and as high

as the bright moon in the sky. I was trying to play it cool. As I opened the front door, I saw old Hobin standing right there waiting for me. I knew I was in deep trouble.

"You had fun," Hobin said in his deep voice.

"Yeah, it was cool," I said, doing my best to avoid eye contact.

I guess the smell of a marijuana forest gave me away, because as I was heading up the stairs, Hobin leaned in to smell me.

"Step into the office," he said in a harsh tone. Then he grabbed me by the shirt and pulled me close to him and let me have it. "What the f---? I told you about coming in this house

I shut the car door and I was off to college. Life after the system had officially begun.

high. Are you stupid? You want to be a bum? You have something that most people don't have—intelligence! Take it from me—you keep getting high you are going to be a f---ing junkie! Now go upstairs and don't you ever let me see you come in this house like that again!"

Some may say that it wasn't right for Hobin to grab me like that, but I say that some people in the system don't seem to care at all about us kids, and Hobin was one of the rare staff who did. He never abused us, but kept it real and pure, never sugarcoating the truth. He was rough, but he believed in me and always said I had a gleam in my eye.

After that day, I wanted to prove that Hobin was right about me. I was not going to be like my drug-addicted parents. I was smart and I would make it.

As I started doing better in school and checked my behavior, I liked the feeling I got hearing people talk positively about me, like, "Joey's doing good," or, "You from a group home? You don't act like it." I got a thrill from changing people's mind about how group home kids act or look.

Those comments fueled my determination not to follow the book of life that my parents had written: "How to Be a F--- Up." I had made up my mind to write my own book of life.

Growing up poor teaches you one of two things: either you become a compulsive spender when you have money, or you become a tight budgeter. I sometimes wonder if I should have gone to college for accounting, since I can stretch $5 to last a week. But during my first year of college, my bank account was dwindling along with my hope and confidence.

At times I would call the group home to say what's up and I'd get a strange feeling, like the people at the end of the line didn't want to know me anymore and everybody was abandoning me. After a while I stopped calling.

I became a loner and kept to myself at college because I couldn't relate to the kids there. It was a private art school, and most of the students were rich and preppy. They seemed to have no idea how to relate to kids like me, and I had no idea how to relate to them.

One typical time I was in my dorm and I overheard one kid say to another, "I was so pissed off at my mom 'cause she wouldn't let me hold the credit card!" I thought to myself, "If that's the worst of your problems, let's trade lives!"

I would have dropped out of college during my first year if it wasn't for my mentor, Jennifer. I'd call her, saying, "Look, Jen, I feel like I'm wasting my time in this school. I would be much better off getting a job and living in my own apartment."

"Yeah, OK, Joe," she'd say. "You think a minimum wage job is the way to live? You gotta be kidding me! You're way too smart for that kind of life. Now call your advisor and sign up for the next semester!"

She had more belief in me than I had in myself. We had the same conversation semester after semester until I got so close to graduating that I was only a few steps away from reaching my goal.

But for a long time, I still believed people at my school looked at me as an outsider. I knew I had to change this. The only way I was going to feel good about myself was to find a way to fit in.

One day my college was having a dance. I forced myself to go, telling myself that it would be fine. The music was loud, people were dancing. I found the couple of friends I'd made. Then the DJ announced to the crowd, "Yo! Listen up! We having an open mic in five minutes."

I thought, "I'm going go up there and tear it up, let these kids know who's the best."

"You ready?" the DJ asked. I was nervous as hell, but I grabbed the mic. I'm not sure what I said, but I'd been rapping for years and had a confident swagger. People were staring at me like, "Where did this kid come from?" When I was done, people came up and complimented me on my performance. Damn, I was feeling good.

For weeks after that, random people would come up to me and mention the open mic, like, "Hey, man, you're pretty good at rapping." Every time there was a freestyle or anything having to do with music, they would call me. I finally started to feel comfortable at my school.

For a long time, I believed people at my college looked at me as an outsider. I knew I had to change this.

When I started making music and writing songs, it was as if I had learned a new language and the people that I once could not communicate with understood my new tongue. Instead of being the anti-social kid, I became the kid who others wanted to be around. If they had raps or were singers, they knew I was the man with the music. As I got more involved, I began to feel like part of something and less alone.

Through music, I also met two guys who became my good friends, Sulton and Razi. Other than our interest in music we were like night and day. Sulton and Razi both came from middle class backgrounds, but they never judged me for being poor. Instead, they seemed to respect me for managing to conquer my crazy life. Over time, we became comfortable with our differences. I realized I didn't have to have the same background as somebody for us to get along.

College never did get easy, but as time went by I learned how to handle the tremendous stress. I worked, stayed focused on school, hung out with my friends, and eventually made it through.

On graduation day I had only $20 in my pocket but I felt like a million bucks. My sister Melissa, my guidance counselor, and my ex-girlfriend were all there. The graduation was at Lincoln Center (the world-renowned music center), where everything was real proper. I had on a collared blue shirt with some nice slacks and spit-shined shoes.

It felt like another four years passed before they announced the graduates. Finally the main speaker finished his long "I want to save the world" speech and said the words I wanted to hear: "May the graduating class please rise."

Oh boy, I was so eager to take that walk across the stage, shake the funny-looking white dude's hand, and do back flips down to my seat. But when my name was finally called, I got real serious.

As I received my degree, I thought about how hard I had worked to get there. I felt that I was what they call "a success story." I wanted to say to everybody who hadn't believed in me, "Look what I did! And you thought I couldn't do it! Ha!" Then I faced the crowd and pumped my degree in the air.

Joseph was 25 when he wrote this story.
After college, he worked in video editing.

Take Our Advice:
Adjusting to College

"My first couple of days, I was like, 'Do I belong here?' Because, I kid you not, there were kids talking about this book they'd read and that philosopher they like. But while they were very intellectual, they were also very, 'Yeah, let's go out and party.' I like to go out but I don't drink. So it was kind of like, 'Where do I fit in here?'

"For me, just seeing my grades made me feel like I belonged. I came to realize that maybe they were feeling insecure like I was and maybe that was why they decided, well, let me bring up everything that I ever learned—ever—to impress people."

—**Desiree**, 19, sophomore

"I'm from New York and I went all the way down to New Orleans to volunteer, and on a whim I decided to stay for college. I don't think I took into account the distance. I had no family around there and there were times when I was just so lonely, so confused.

"To deal with it, first I cried, and then I remembered why I'd come—to get an education, to learn about myself and the world. And if you stay focused on why you came to college, then you should be OK."

—**Tasha**, 20, sophomore

"During my first month of college, I felt that none of my professors were going to like my work because I had no clue what I was doing. I worried so much about getting negative feedback from my professors that it would keep me from finishing my assignments. I had to learn to speak up and ask questions when I was unsure of something instead of waiting until it was too late.

—*Pedro*, 21, sophomore

"The hardest thing for me about adjusting to college has been the writing. In high school, it was easy for me to get A's and B's on essays, but in college I've been getting C+'s. I didn't understand why. Now I go to tutoring and ask friends to read over my essays, and my writing is improving."

—*Teyu*, 18, freshman

"Social life in high school was all about fitting in with the crowd, gossiping and fighting. Boring! In college things have a more moderate tone and nobody broadcasts other people's business enough to make it a big deal. Thank God for that, eh?

—*Otis*, 19, freshman

"In high school, whether I spoke up in class or not really didn't make a difference. But in college I've made a 180-degree transformation. I've started raising my hand, I get into class debates, and sometimes even challenge the teacher when I think it's necessary. Participation counts in college."

—*Teyu*, 18, freshman

From 'Group Home Child' to College Success

By Tamecka L. Crawford

Going off to college for the first time can be a scary experience for anyone, but especially for a foster child. We don't have the support of a parent, and a lot of times we feel as if we're alone in the world. Before I left for Sullivan County Community College in upstate New York, I started to worry about what college life would be like for me.

Although I wanted so badly to be independent, I still wanted someone there to fall back on. How would I survive all alone in a strange place? Also, could I make it as a "college student"? Would I fail or drop out? I worried about people finding out I was in a group home and treating me differently or making fun of me. I even wondered if my professors would treat me differently.

Although I had gone on several college tours and seen the campus of my school before I went there, I was still nervous. I was anxious to know if I would be compatible with my roommate, or if we would have problems.

When I first started classes, things seemed fine. I had six classes and the workload was all right. But after a little while I met a guy and started spending lots of time with him, skipping classes and not studying. I felt I had all the time in the world to pull my grades up. So I slowed down and started missing classes that I didn't like. I began having trouble, and my grades dropped tremendously in history and math.

My roommate would talk on the phone with her mother, describing her day and her classes. I wished so badly that could be my mother.

I found myself using the excuse of being in foster care every time I missed a class or failed an exam. A lot of times I would say to myself, "Oh, I'm in a group home. Who cares if I go to class or not, or if I failed an exam or even if I passed one?"

I felt as if the words "group home child" were hanging over my head. Even though nobody treated me differently, in the back of my mind I felt they were. Like at the financial aid office, I felt that they were hesitant to deal with me because they knew I was in foster care.

My self-esteem was very low my first semester. I sometimes just gave up and didn't care. As a result, I completed my first semester with a 1.0 grade point average (about a D average), and ended up on academic probation my second semester.

I felt nobody cared for me, and it showed. I felt this way because I didn't have any family support. I kept making the mistake of comparing my life to students who had parents calling often and coming to visit them, sending them care packages filled with all sorts of things, including their favorite foods, money, and supplies they asked for. I wanted so badly to have someone care about me like that.

I felt neglected, not to mention jealous. I remember hearing my roommate talk on the phone with her mother, describing her day and what classes she liked more than others. I wished so badly that could be my mother or somebody who really cared for me. Although I did stay in contact with people from my former group home and with my junior high school dean, it wasn't a substitute for family.

Just before the end of the first semester I realized that I had wasted time feeling sorry for myself and had to do something about it. I never thought the semester would go so quickly. Like I said before, when you first get to college you think you have all this time, then before you know it, it's over.

Gradually I realized that time was passing me by and nobody was going to care for me until I cared for myself. I was so wrapped up in worrying about having people do things for me and care for me that I wasn't taking the time to care for myself.

I got tired of using the fact that I was in foster care as an excuse.

I got tired of using the fact that I was in foster care as an excuse. I was tired of failing my exams. I was tired of crying. At the same time, I also noticed that the people that I was envying weren't doing so well in their classes, either.

I finally understood that it wasn't because I was in foster care that I was failing my classes. It was because I had been paying too much attention to what people thought of me and how they treated me, and too little to my school work. I had to accept the fact that I was in foster care and move on. It wasn't being in a group home that was holding me back—it was me.

After spring break, I finally decided to wipe my eyes and find ways to start my independent life. The first thing I did was to attend all my classes Monday morning and start pulling my grades up.

In my second semester my grade point average shot up to

3.25. I was studying night and day, especially subjects like history, which I always had problems with. I went to a tutor who worked with me and I also found peer tutors (fellow college students who were good in a particular subject) to help me. In exchange, I'd type a paper for them or make them dinner.

I started letting professors know I was having problems and some of them would meet with me privately to help me. Or if they saw that I was struggling they would let me know by saying, "I see that your grades are dropping again. Are you having trouble studying?" Some of them would give me new study methods or extra material to use.

Just like in a group home, when you're in college you have to do things for yourself and make sure things are getting done to help you.

My next step was to get counseling. When you're on academic probation you automatically get group counseling. I'd had counseling in the group home, but I never liked it because I felt we were pre-judged. But in college I decided it would also help to have a one-on-one counselor because I realized I needed help dealing with the transition from the group home to college life.

I had a nice female counselor who listened to me talk about school, my group homes, and other things on my mind. At the end of the sessions she would give suggestions on how to deal with my problems. It helped me realize that even if I couldn't have the family relationships that I wanted so badly, I could thank God for the people who were taking the time out to help me any way they could.

I also got a part-time job to make some extra money when the group home couldn't help me pay for whatever I needed. I even managed to put some money in the bank for rainy days. Basically, I started trying not to depend on the system too much. By my third semester in school I was no longer seeking as much support from the agency or my caseworker. I was trying to make it on my own.

I continued to go to counseling because I found it a very big help. Through counseling, I realized that just because people live with their biological families does not automatically make their lifestyle better than mine. I also realized that in some ways being a foster child was an advantage for me.

For example, living in a group home turned out to be a big help in adjusting to college life because I'd already learned how to live with different people's personalities and attitudes. Also, I already had a sense of independence. Just like in a group home, when you're in college you have to do things for yourself and make sure things are getting done to help you.

One thing that was easier for me about the group home was that everyone has something in common: your family can't or won't take care of you. You all understand that and can talk about it with each other. But in college you meet people from all sorts of different backgrounds, and sometimes you feel envious of their lifestyles. When other students were planning their spring breaks in Hawaii or Virginia, I was deciding on what movie I was going to see during the break, or whether to go visit a relative or just stay in the group home.

I learned that in order for anything to change, I first must care about myself. Then I'll be able to care about the situation and do what I need to so I can be successful.

Tamecka was 21 when she wrote this story.

Take Our Advice:
Dealing with Distractions

"My extracurricular activities distract me. All the clubs seem so awesome. It's good to get involved in campus groups, but at the same time you really have to focus on your schoolwork."

—*Janill*, 21, senior

"Dorm life can be a distraction. There are always people around. At 3 a.m., you have a paper to write and everyone's just so interesting. My room was right outside the elevator so everyone came barging in all the time. It was really hard to get stuff done. I had to sneak away to the library one time."

—*Desiree*, 19, sophomore

"Parties! You get all these party invites and you're like, 'Yeah! I'm gonna go clubbing and I'm gonna write this paper tonight—of course I can do that!' You can't do that.

—*Tasha*, 20, sophomore

Females are much different in college than they were in high school. They know what they want to achieve in life. They don't focus on boys, they don't have loud outbursts, and they have a greater vocabulary as well as vision for their lives. They motivate me, but it's distracting because I start focusing on them instead of class.

—*Pedro*, 21, sophomore

Freshman Blues

By Matthew Dedewo

As far as college was concerned, I must have made every mistake in the book. I thought the first semester was supposed to be the hardest, but to my surprise it was my second semester when things took a turn for the worse.

Before I even started college classes, I was already having a hard time. I didn't know there were so many bureaucratic procedures, so I was late with everything, including my financial aid forms and my tuition payment.

I was also late with registration and that added to my stress, because the only classes I could get into conflicted with my work schedule. Back then I was working full-time. My job was willing to be flexible, but I still ended up having the harder classes at night, after a long day's work, and the easier classes in the morning, when I was most alert. So lots of times I was feeling sleepy when I needed to be wide awake, and I was wasting my mental alertness on subjects I could've passed in my sleep.

Once classes started, I didn't apply myself enough. I had been out of school for a couple of years, and high school had been such a breeze that I underestimated college work. My first semester classes didn't require much study time. I passed them with C's and a couple of B's, except for a math class, which I failed.

High school had been such a breeze that I underestimated college work.

Second semester was harder. During the beginning of the semester, I got in the habit of taking a couple of hours out of each day to study, but I was still struggling with that one math class. And even though it was my second time taking it, I didn't want to get a tutor. I was too proud.

Then the subject I'd planned to major in started to frustrate me. I liked to draw and as a child when I was asked what I wanted to be when I grew up, I always said an architect. I knew there was a lot of drawing involved, but I didn't expect to spend hours and hours drawing the same thing over and over from different perspectives.

During the first semester, I had felt proud that I was finally pursuing what I thought was my life's dream, even though the classes were a little dull. But by the second semester, the subject seemed tedious and I felt like I was forcing myself to do it. When I found out that not all architects make as much money as I thought they did, I realized that I needed another life dream. That's when I stopped trying to be the best I could be and started slacking off in my classes.

Soon things really began to fall apart. I was already working full time but then I took on a part-time job for extra money. The room I was renting was too far from the school, so I found a studio apartment only 30 minutes away where I could live alone. But that meant more rent and thus more hours at work. I gave up my social life, and I was soon overwhelmed. I started missing classes because it was a lot cheaper than missing a shift at work. I needed a roof over my head more than I needed the college credits, especially since I wasn't going to immediately reap the benefits of college.

Next, some of my financial aid was taken away—financial aid will be taken away for bad grades and poor attendance, and I had both—and the school sent me the bill. I wasn't able to pay it right then so it affected my credit report. (By the time I was able to pay it back, a year had passed and it had been sent to a collection agency, which is a company whose sole purpose is to bug debtors like me until we pay up.)

Needless to say, by the middle of my second semester, I was overwhelmed and frustrated. It was hard to juggle work and school, and my low grades and new debt made me feel like a failure. At the time, it never occurred to me to speak to a counselor or even to go to school part-time and ease the burden. I was used to doing things my way even if it was the hard way—

I'm going to be more careful this time. The moment I feel myself falling behind I'm going to get a tutor.

although if I had swallowed my pride and asked for help, I'm sure things would've turned out differently. Instead, I decided to give up on my second semester. I wasn't quitting, I told myself. I was just going to take a little while to get myself into a better situation.

That was over two years ago and I'm just now going back to college. I worked for half a year at a job that turned out to be not so hot, and then I spent two years in the Navy. Even though the Navy taught me a lot, I still feel like I'm behind in the schedule I had planned for my life. At the age of 26 I should be working on getting my master's degree, not my associate's degree.

That gives me the urge to overload myself with classes trying to catch up, but this time I'm going to be careful not to add that to my list of mistakes. I've decided to major in computer engineering and networking. It's a profession that's in demand and it will give me the freedom of working with a firm while also freelance for extra income.

I'm going to be more careful about my class schedule and the moment I feel myself falling behind, I'm going to get a tutor. I plan to go full-time, but I'm willing to go part-time if things get too tough.

I don't expect my previous experience to make things that much easier—I'm sure I still have a few more mistakes to make. But I understand now that college is a learning experience just like life; the only way to fail is to give up.

---

*Matthew went on to graduate from
New York City College of Technology.*

Take Our Advice:
Managing Your Time

"I see a lot of older people at my school. I took a class with this woman who has three kids and works a full-time job, and she still goes to school. So I know if she can do that and get good grades, then I can certainly do it."

—*Pauline*, 21, junior

"I write everything in my planner. I can't function without one. I always transfer everything from the syllabus to my planner, otherwise I'll forget."

—*Janill*, 21, senior

"In our dorm rooms, our closet doors are made out of mirrors, so I just wrote everything I had to do on the mirror with a dry-erase marker. It washes off. I see it every morning when I open my closet. It's a good system."

—*Tasha*, 20, sophomore

"At first I became so overwhelmed with my assignments that it began to wear me down. I've handled it by going to study hall and using my free time to study. Why fight with yourself when you could get the help that's right under your nose in the tutoring center or the college library?"

—*Ashunte*, 20, freshman

"It's obvious who is and who is not studying. You'll realize that when you see your class shrinking, when you see the same people come in late to class or leave class early like they did in high school. Don't be one of them."

—*Pedro*, 21, sophomore

"I fixed my time management problem by using a planner where I arranged my appointments, my classes, and my free time. A friend also gave me a great piece of advice: do your college assignments during times of day when you feel energetic, and save e-mails and Facebook for right before you go to bed when you feel exhausted."

—*Teyu*, 18, freshman

"When I get home, I shower, eat, lie down, and read. And in the morning I'll come to work a little early or stay a little later and read up."

—*Hector*, 22, sophomore

Jessica Deng

Freshman Year 101: How to Survive

Once you're in college, it often takes a while to get your bearings. Here are some things college students often have to learn the hard way:

• **Get to know your academic advisor.** This person's job is to make sure you are earning credits toward a degree so that you get through college quickly and successfully. Don't limit visits to one-time course planning and credit counts. Ask them questions over e-mail, and schedule extra visits during the semester if you need help.

• **Take a balanced course load.** All students struggle to adjust to the demands of college. If you take a tough class, try to balance it with something you feel more confident about.

Working with your academic advisors and professors, find

out if you're ready for specific classes by asking about prerequisites and workload.

• **Talk to professors.** New college students often feel intimidated by professors. But your professors are there to help you succeed, and they can become valuable mentors who might help you get a job down the road. Some professors are more helpful than others. But it's important to get to know all of them. Talk to them after class, go to their office hours, and ask questions.

• **Get help.** Colleges have many programs to help you with academics and career planning. Get familiar with all the student services programs so you know where to go when you need help. Don't wait until you're drowning to seek help with tough classes. Instead, make an appointment with a tutor at the beginning of the semester to learn about the services they offer. Visit the career center to get advice on career planning, from building a professional résumé to internships and job-hunting.

Don't wait until you're drowning to seek help with tough classes.

• **Be disciplined.** Unlike high school, no one is going to nag you to finish your homework or go to class. College classes move fast, so use your time wisely. Make yourself a weekly schedule with plenty of blocks of time for studying.

• **Familiarize yourself with the financial aid office.** If you're having trouble paying for books or other basic needs, make an appointment to talk with a financial aid adviser.

Take the time to carefully review and understand your financial aid package—What exactly does it pay for? Do you have to do work-study? How much are you expected to pay out of your own pocket?

- **Make a personal budget and stick to it.** It's easy to dig yourself into a financial hole. Make a list of all your expenses, and what financial aid will and won't pay for. Also keep in mind that financial aid may be delayed. If this happens, talk to the financial aid office right away.

  Don't wait until you're in danger of failing classes because you haven't been able to buy books, or you haven't attended class because you don't have money for bus fare.

- **Try new things.** College can be lonely in the beginning. It might feel as if you've been thrown into a whole new world with people very different from yourself. But it's also a great opportunity to re-invent yourself and make new friends.

  Consider joining clubs and volunteering. Visit the campus activities office to learn about low-cost trips and events.

- **Take care of yourself.** The transition to college is physically and emotionally stressful. Exercise, eat well, get plenty of sleep, and don't hesitate to use the campus health center when you're not feeling your best. Counselors can help you through the stress and emotional turmoil—they've heard it all. Know your limits, too: risky behaviors and too much partying can bring you down fast and put you in dangerous situations.

Take Our Advice:
Making the Most of Academics

"As I began to read more in college, my vocabulary increased. Now I can comprehend better and I have a clearer idea of how to write. The more you read, the more you will understand words and how to put them together in the right form."

—*Pedro*, 21, sophomore

"Lecture halls are huge, and sometimes you don't hear well in the back. I always try to stay right at the front so that I can hear the professor. Lecture can be intimidating when you don't understand something. In my mind, it was like, 'I don't really want to ask something in front of 300 people when it might be an obvious thing.' But as semesters went along I got better and better at it. I didn't really care. It's my grade; I ask whatever I want."

—*Janill*, 21, senior

"I advise forming study groups because learning as a group and asking questions is more effective than just reading the textbook over and over again. You're more likely to understand the concepts and less likely to fall asleep when you interact with others."

—*Teyu*, 18, freshman

"Going to a professor's office hours is the best way to get help. Not only will you get answers straight from the source, it tells your professor that you are taking the class seriously and you are doing your best."

—*Te-Li*, 20, junior

"If there are any doubts in your mind when you're trying to pick a major—and there will be lots of doubts as to what you want to do—talk to your academic adviser. That was really helpful to me."

—*Desiree*, 19, sophomore

"Build a relationship with your teacher. If you're having trouble, go to them and say, 'OK, I know I'm failing and I know I have to pick up the slack. How can I do this?' Some teachers say if you fail you fail. But if you build up a relationship with them there's more of a chance you can do it. If you don't make yourself known, they're not going to know you. I don't shut up in class now."

—*Hector*, 22, sophomore

Study Strategies

Keeping up with readings

When you're reading, don't just highlight! Instead:

1) Outline as you read: begin by skimming through the reading to see what the major topics and sub-sections might be. Then read the material more slowly than usual and write your outline of the major points as you read along.

OR:

2) Break down the reading material into smaller, more digestible sections. After each small section, close the book and write down what the important points are (in your own words). Before going on to the next section, reread to check your facts and to be sure you didn't miss anything. This method allows you to read whole sections without having to stop to write your outline. Have a dictionary handy to look up the meaning and pronunciation of words you're unfamiliar with.

Prepping for exams

1) Organization: Make sure you are keeping up with the weekly readings. Organize your notes from class and from your readings. Do not rely on just one or the other; incorporate both.

2) Study groups: Form study groups of three to four people. Take turns assuming the role of "teacher," explaining certain points to the others in the group.

3) Flash Cards: Write the word/concept/idea on one side of an index card and write the definition/explanation/example on the other side. Then test yourself as you are waiting on line, on lunch breaks, riding the subway, etc.

4) Start Early: Do NOT cram the night before. Start studying as early as possible. Take advantage of professors' office hours if you have any questions, as there may not be time for review during class.

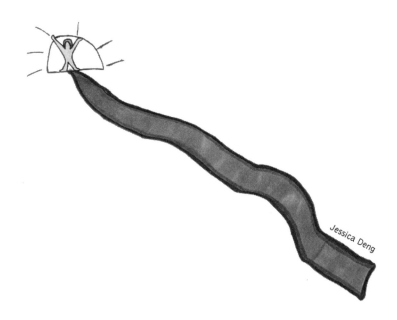

Jessica Deng

Where There's a Will, There's a Way

By Merli Desrosier

I always knew I wanted to go to college and get a degree. It was embedded in my mind that the only way to get out of a bad situation was through school, and I wanted to go to Purchase College, a public school in New York State. I had read about the college and visited the campus. I loved the atmosphere and being able to meet other people from around the world. But getting to Purchase was not so easy.

My first obstacle was that I wasn't a legal U.S. resident (I didn't have a green card), so I wouldn't get financial aid and I would get charged tuition at the international rate. My agency would only put up $1,000, which wouldn't even cover part-time tuition.

Then I found out about a law that said if you could show

proof that you went to high school in the state the year before applying to college, that you would be able to pay the resident tuition rate instead of the international rate. So I got in under that. I still didn't have any financial aid, though so I applied and was accepted at the College of Staten Island here in New York City, which is less expensive. My agency put up the $1,000 and the rest of the money came from a sponsor.

My first semester I did great. But second semester, the agency wasn't willing to put up money again for my tuition. It was a one-shot thing. So I started working to pay for school.

I couldn't handle having to work full time and afterward traveling 2 ½ hours to class.

That's when everything went downhill. I went from about a 3.5 GPA down to a 2.2. At the same time, I was moved into an independent living program in the Bronx, where I shared an apartment with another young person who'd been in foster care. But my new apartment was so far away from school. I couldn't handle having to work full-time and afterward traveling 2 ½ hours to class in Staten Island.

Then I broke my ankle and couldn't get to class. It was too late in the semester to drop classes, so I was placed on academic probation. And on top of everything, I was about to age out of foster care.

About three months after I aged out, I finally got my green card, which made me eligible for financial aid. So I went back to the College of Staten Island. They set a deadline for me to bring up my GPA, but I was still working full time, and I couldn't take as many classes as they required. I ended up getting dismissed from the college.

My only option at that point was one local college where they would transfer credits without transferring the grades. That meant I could start my GPA over and still keep some credits.

I wasn't sure if I wanted to go to this school because it had a bad reputation. But at that point, an old social worker came back into my life and encouraged me to go, improve my GPA, and transfer later. She offered to pay my expenses out of her own pocket if I kept a B average. I agreed, and that enabled me to stop working. I just went to school.

My first semester, I got a 3.2 average. A year later, I got my associate's degree. So yeah, not working helps out! I finished up that year with a 3.5 average with honors, and I finally got accepted to Purchase College. It was a long road, but I made it.

Merli later graduated from Purchase College.

Take Our Advice:
Financial Tips

"Have a good relationship with the financial aid office staff. Say hi to them every once in a while. Tell them, 'Your hair looks nice today.' When they have to do the paperwork, they might be more likely to go the extra mile for you."

—*Pauline*, 21, junior

- -

"If you need to go to the college financial aid office, get there early—as if you were buying concert tickets. If you have a class that starts at 10 a.m. and you get on that line at 9, chances are you're not going to make it to class that day."

—*Hector*, 22, sophomore

"If you don't know what you're doing or if a financial aid counselor isn't helping you, go to someone else."

—*Tasha*, 20, sophomore

"I have a checking account with online access, so it's easy for me to see how much money I have and think about how much of it I should spend. I also write down all my expenses in a balance booklet so I can see how I'm spending my money. I think college students should have a bank account, because cash can be easily stolen and it's more tempting to spend it. But be careful about going to other banks' ATMs because banks often charge big fees when you don't use your own bank's ATM."

—**Teyu**, 18, freshman

"Too many people, me included, spend money on things they want but don't really need. It's always a good idea to save extra money for books or other things you need unexpectedly."

—**Otis**, 19, freshman

"Budget your money carefully. Before buying something, ask yourself, 'Do I really need it?' and, 'How will this benefit me?'"

—**Te-Li**, 20, junior

Jessica Deng

Community College:
A Second Chance

By Jordan Temple

I used to think community colleges were just a fall-back option if you completely bombed in high school. That's kind of what happened to me, actually. I attended four different high schools over four years, and I chose to clown around instead of doing my work. I was a know-it-all with false confidence. I felt that because of my strong grades in middle school and freshman year of high school, I was in the clear to meander through the halls instead of attending class.

I finally got my act together at my fifth high school, John V. Lindsay Wildcat Academy, a school that helps kids catch up on their credits and improve their grades. If it wasn't for that school, which pulled me in and helped me graduate, I'd probably be in a dead-end job instead of pursuing a career.

I knew that I wanted to go to college last year when I started getting my grades up. I felt better about myself and I had a good sense of what I should be doing—furthering my education. Over a year and a half, I worked to earn credits and improve my grades at Wildcat Academy. Finally, last January, I graduated high school.

When my guidance counselor suggested I look through the SUNY (State University of New York) handbook to see which two-year colleges I might like to attend, I felt regretful that I didn't have the grades to go to a four-year college.

I felt like I'd been given a clean slate. Now I could become more of an individual instead of keeping up my slacker image.

But I was glad I could attend college, period. I figured that if I worked hard and managed my money I could transfer to a four-year college and leave with a bachelor's degree, accumulating less debt than I would have if I'd gone to a four-year college the whole time.

I was relieved when I found out that some SUNY community colleges had dorms, because I wanted to get out of New York City, meet new people, and get the entire college experience. I wanted fresh air and a change of scenery, away from the distractions of city life and friends.

I eventually settled on Onondaga Community College in Syracuse, one of the largest community colleges in central New York. There are 9,000 day students and 500 students who live in dormitories. The college's website and virtual tour of the dorms blew me away, and so did the quality of the professors.

I met professors at an open house and it made it that much easier for me to choose Onondaga over the three other community colleges that I was accepted to. I was interested in communications, and the teachers explained what courses would benefit me and what careers I could pursue with that major (like marketing, public relations, or teaching). Plus, my credits would easily transfer to a four-year college after two years.

When I first got there, I was really shy and kept to myself. But I grew to like living in the dorms and meeting people. Students were friendly. They held doors for each other from about 20 feet away, and said hello.

I also liked the academic scene. I felt like I'd been given a clean slate. Now I could become more of an individual instead of keeping up my slacker image.

I took four classes my first semester: interpersonal communication, English, oceanography, and a class about college study habits. My professor for that class was stern but cool. He was a middle-aged African-American man whose Afrocentricity rivaled my mother's.

He had posters of Malcolm X in his office and wore dashikis (traditional African garb) to class. We spoke about my grades, what classes I enjoyed, my major, issues in the black community, and my favorite sport, baseball. It was nice to have a professor I could talk to.

I found ways to have intercultural communication as well. I was interested in clubs that brought people together. At Onondaga, I found two that did just that. I joined the ESL (English as a Second Language) mentoring program, where an American-born student is paired with an international student. You meet twice a week to share your cultures, opinions, and questions, and talk about college life.

I was paired with Seung Young Kim, a student from Korea. We talked about the difference between North and South Korea, Korean celebrities, and America's favorite pastime (and mine): baseball. We became good friends and learned a lot from each other.

I also joined the JAAMA club, a club that promotes unity

among African-Americans on campus and shares ideas about issues in the black community. In the fall, I'm going to run for student representative, which would mean I'd be responsible for getting money for the club at student government meetings and recruiting more people to join.

Most importantly, I figured out my study habits. I found that the library is where I am most focused. I practically lived there my first semester. My plan is to get my grades up and then transfer to a four-year college. Many Onondaga students transfer to Syracuse University after two years, and I hope that I can do the same.

If I worked hard and managed my money I could transfer, accumulating less debt than at a four-year college.

Even if I don't get into Syracuse, I want to attend a four-year college that has a good speech communication program, a marketing and business program, and a center for aspiring entrepreneurs.

One day I'd like to become a baseball scout and, eventually, general manager of a baseball team. I also want to start a nonprofit to fund low-income kids to go to baseball camp. I want to start an initiative to get more blacks back in baseball—in front offices, on major league teams, playing abroad, scouting, and playing minor league ball. A background in business and marketing would help me with that.

But for now, my focus is school. This fall I hope to maintain a 3.3 GPA or higher. I also would like to be more outgoing and attend more school events, go to a party or two, and contribute to a poetry slam. I developed a passion for writing poems my first semester. I thought a lot at school, and I started wanting to write down my thoughts (in between essays and homework).

I'm glad I embraced the idea of community college even though I had my doubts about it at first. College has been a great experience so far. I feel a lot more at peace with myself now. I know who I am: a kid who loves to read and learn new things (and is obsessed with baseball). I can see the purpose in everything that I do now, and how doing well in the present will help solidify my future. Community college hasn't been a disappointment, but a second chance.

Jordan was 19 when he wrote this story.

College Resources

College Board
www.collegeboard.com
This site has tons of information on college planning/preparation, financial aid, and college success.

The Free Application for Federal Student Aid (FAFSA)
www.fafsa.ed.gov
The FAFSA is the first step to receiving any kind of federal aid and can be completed online at this site. The website lists FAFSA application deadlines state by state and answers basic questions you might have about your eligibility.

www.finaid.org
This amazing website gives tips on filling out your FAFSA, provides a guide to the very diverse world of private scholarships (including scholarships for "skateboard activists," left-handed people, and obese students). It also gives information on student loans and how to avoid scholarship scams, and has a special section for students interested in careers in the military.

Go College
www.gocollege.com
Click on the College Survival section. It covers grades, college social life, money management, health, and more.

Know How 2 Go
www.knowhow2go.org
This site breaks down the college preparation process by grade level for high school students.

National Center for Education Statistics

www.nces.ed.gov/collegenavigator

Look up any school you're interested to find out all kinds of information, including tuition and fees, what kinds of financial aid is offered, a race and gender breakdown of the student body, on-campus crime rates, graduation rates, and more.

National College Access Network

www.collegeaccess.org

To find a college access program near you, click on the "National College Access Program Directory," under the Resources button on their homepage. You can locate programs by typing in your zip code.

Orphan Foundation of America

www.orphan.org

At this website, you can apply for lots of different financial aid that is designated to help current and former foster youth get an education. The Orphan Foundation of America gives out Education and Training Vouchers for seven different states, and also gives out Casey Scholarships.

Teens:
How to Get More Out of This Book

Self-help: The teens who wrote the stories in this book did so because they hope that telling their stories will help readers who are facing similar challenges. They want you to know that you are not alone, and that taking specific steps can help you manage or overcome very difficult situations. They've done their best to be clear about the actions that worked for them so you can see if they'll work for you.

Writing: You can also use the book to improve your writing skills. Each teen in this book wrote 5-10 drafts of his or her story before it was published. If you read the stories closely you'll see that the teens work to include a beginning, a middle, and an end, and good scenes, description, dialogue, and anecdotes (little stories). To improve your writing, take a look at how these writers construct their stories. Try some of their techniques in your own writing.

How to Use This Book in Staff Training

Staff say that reading these stories gives them greater insight into what teens are thinking and feeling, and new strategies for working with them. You can help the staff you work with by using these stories as case studies.

Select one story to read in the group, and ask staff to identify and discuss the main issue facing the teen. There may be disagreement about this, based on the background and experience of staff. That is fine. One point of the exercise is that teens have complex lives and needs. Adults can probably be more effective if they don't focus too narrowly and can see several dimensions of their clients.

Ask staff: What issues or feelings does the story provoke in them? What kind of help do they think the teen wants? What interventions are likely to be most promising? Least effective? Why? How would you build trust with the teen writer? How have other adults failed the teen, and how might that affect his or her willingness to accept help? What other resources would be helpful to this teen, such as peer support, a mentor, counseling, family therapy, etc?

Discussion Guide

Teachers and Staff:
How to Use This Book in Groups

When working with teens individually or in groups, you can use these stories to help young people face difficult issues in a way that feels safe to them. That's because talking about the issues in the stories usually feels safer to teens than talking about those same issues in their own lives. Addressing issues through the stories allows for some personal distance; they hit close to home, but not too close. Talking about them opens up a safe place for reflection. As teens gain confidence talking about the issues in the stories, they usually become more comfortable talking about those issues in their own lives.

Below are general questions to guide your discussion. In most cases you can read a story and conduct a discussion in one 45-minute session. Teens are usually happy to read the stories aloud, with each teen reading a paragraph or two. (Allow teens to pass if they don't want to read.) It takes 10-15 minutes to read a story straight through. However, it is often more effective to let workshop participants make comments and discuss the story as you go along. The workshop leader may even want to annotate her copy of the story beforehand with key questions.

If teens read the story ahead of time or silently, it's good to break the ice with a few questions that get everyone on the same page: Who is the main character? How old is she? What happened to her? How did she respond? Another good starting question is: "What stood out for you in the story?" Go around the room and let each person briefly mention one thing.

Then move on to open-ended questions, which encourage participants to think more deeply about what the writers were feeling, the choices they faced, and the actions they took. There are no right or wrong answers to the open-ended questions.

Open-ended questions encourage participants to think about how the themes, emotions, and choices in the stories relate to their own lives. Here are some examples of open-ended questions that we have found to be effective. You can use variations of these questions with almost any story in this book.

—What main problem or challenge did the writer face?

—What choices did the teen have in trying to deal with the problem?

—Which way of dealing with the problem was most effective for the teen? Why?

—What strengths, skills, or resources did the teen use to address the challenge?

—If you were in the writer's shoes, what would you have done?

—What could adults have done better to help this young person?

—What have you learned by reading this story that you didn't know before?

—What, if anything, will you do differently after reading this story?

—What surprised you in this story?

—Do you have a different view of this issue, or see a different way of dealing with it, after reading this story? Why or why not?

Credits

**The stories in this book originally appeared in the following
Youth Communication publications:**

"Learning to Believe in Myself," by Ja'Nelle Earle, *Represent*, May/June 2005; "I Plan to Go to College—What About the Other Foster Teens?" by Luis Reyes, *Represent*, January/February 2002; "Stressed For Success," by Rana Sino, *Represent*, January/February 2002; "Can You Get to College With a GED?" by Samantha Flowers, *Represent*, March/April 2009; "Delaying College Helped Me Grow," by Jarel Melendez, *Represent*, September/October 2008; "Left in the Dark," by Shameka Vincent, *Represent*, September/October 2008; "Staying On Track During Senior Year," *Represent*, September/October 2008; "How I Overcame My Fear of Applying," by Debra Samuels, *Represent*, September/October 1994; "Bookin' It for the SAT," by Hattie Rice, *Represent*, May/June 2005; "How to Write a College Essay," by Esther Rajavelu, *New Youth Connections*, December 1995; "Four Easy Steps to a Pre-College Plan," *Represent*, September/October 2008; "Questions Every College-Bound Student Should Ask," by Latonya M. Pogue, *New Youth Connections*, December 1995; "My College Fantasies," by Merli Desrosier, *Represent*, January/February 2002; "Where the Money's At," by James Davis, *Represent*, January/February 2000; "Five Common Myths About Financial Aid," by Felisha Lewis, *Represent*, November/December 1997; "Financial Aid 101," *Represent*, May/June 2005; "The College of My Dreams… With No Money Down," by Lishoné Bowsky, *Represent*, January/February 2002; "How a Green Card Helps You Pay for College," by Leana, *Represent*, May/June 1996; "How To Get a Green Card," by Theresa Hughes, *Represent*, July/August 2006; "There's Always a Choice," by Xavier Reyes, *Represent*, September/October 2008; "Me vs. The World," by Joseph Alvarez, *Represent*, May/June 2005; "From 'Group Home Child' to College Success," by Tamecka L. Crawford, *Represent*, July/August 2003; "Freshman Blues," by Matthew Dedewo, *Represent*, January/February 2002; "Freshman Year 101: How to Survive," *Represent*, September/October 2008; "Where There's a Will, There's a Way," by Merli Desrosier, *Represent*, September/October 2008; "Community College: A Second Chance," by Jordan Temple, *New Youth Connections*, September/October, 2008.

About
Youth Communication

Youth Communication, founded in 1980, is a nonprofit youth development program located in New York City whose mission is to teach writing, journalism, and leadership skills. The teenagers we train become writers for our websites and books and for two print magazines: *New Youth Connections*, a general-interest youth magazine, and *Represent*, a magazine by and for young people in foster care.

Each year, up to 100 young people participate in Youth Communication's after school and summer journalism workshops, where they work under the direction of full-time professional editors. Most are African-American, Latino, or Asian, and many are recent immigrants. The opportunity to reach their peers with accurate portrayals of their lives and important self-help information motivates the young writers to create powerful stories.

Our goal is to run a strong youth development program in which teens produce high quality stories that inform and inspire their peers. Doing so requires us to be sensitive to the complicated lives and emotions of the teen participants while also providing an intellectually rigorous experience. We achieve that goal in the writing/teaching/editing relationship, which is the core of our program.

Our teaching and editorial process begins with discussions

between adult editors and the teen staff. In those meetings, the teens and the editors work together to identify the most important issues in the teens' lives and to figure out how those issues can be turned into stories that will resonate with teen readers.

Once story topics are chosen, students begin the process of crafting their stories. For a personal story, that means revisiting events in one's past to understand their significance for the future. For a commentary, it means developing a logical and persuasive point of view. For a reported story, it means gathering information through research and interviews. Students look inward and outward as they try to make sense of their experiences and the world around them and find the points of intersection between personal and social concerns. That process can take a few weeks or a few months. Stories frequently go through 10 or more drafts as students work under the guidance of their editors, the way any professional writer does.

Many of the students who walk through our doors have uneven skills, as a result of poor education, living under extremely stressful conditions, or coming from homes where English is a second language. Yet, to complete their stories, students must successfully perform a wide range of activities, including writing and rewriting, reading, discussion, reflection, research, interviewing, and typing. They must work as members of a team and they must accept individual responsibility. They learn to provide constructive criticism, and to accept it. They engage in explorations of truthfulness, fairness, and accuracy. They meet deadlines. They must develop the audacity to believe that they have something important to say and the humility to recognize that saying it well is not a process of instant gratification. Rather, it usually requires a long, hard struggle through many discussions and much rewriting.

It would be impossible to teach these skills and dispositions as separate, disconnected topics, like grammar, ethics, or assertiveness. However, we find that students make rapid progress when they are learning skills in the context of an inquiry that is personally significant to them and that will benefit their peers.

When teens publish their stories—in *New Youth Connections* and *Represent,* on the Web, and in other publications—they reach tens of thousands of teen and adult readers. Teachers, counselors, social workers, and other adults circulate the stories to young people in their classes and out-of-school youth programs. Adults tell us that teens in their programs—including many who are ordinarily resistant to reading—clamor for the stories. Teen readers report that the stories give them information they can't get anywhere else, and inspire them to reflect on their lives and open lines of communication with adults.

Writers usually participate in our program for one semester, though some stay much longer. Years later, many of them report that working here was a turning point in their lives—that it helped them acquire the confidence and skills that they needed for success in college and careers. Scores of our graduates have overcome tremendous obstacles to become journalists, writers, and novelists. They include National Book Award finalist and MacArthur Fellowship winner Edwidge Danticat, novelist Ernesto Quiñonez, writer Veronica Chambers, and *New York Times* reporter Rachel Swarns. Hundreds more are working in law, business, and other careers. Many are teachers, principals, and youth workers, and several have started nonprofit youth programs themselves and work as mentors—helping another generation of young people develop their skills and find their voices.

Youth Communication is a nonprofit educational corporation. Contributions are gratefully accepted and are tax deductible to the fullest extent of the law.

To make a contribution, or for information about our publications and programs, including our catalog of over 100 books and curricula for hard-to-reach teens, see www.youthcomm.org.

About the Editors

Autumn Spanne is the editor of *Represent*, Youth Communication's national magazine by and for youth in foster care. Prior to working at Youth Communication, Autumn was a reporter for newspapers in Massachusetts and California and spent five years teaching English and journalism on the Navajo Nation. She has a BA in literature from the University of California, Santa Cruz, an MS in journalism from Columbia University, and an MA in education from Western New Mexico University.

Keith Hefner co-founded Youth Communication in 1980 and has directed it ever since. He is the recipient of the Luther P. Jackson Education Award from the New York Association of Black Journalists and a MacArthur Fellowship. He was also a Revson Fellow at Columbia University.

Laura Longhine is the editorial director at Youth Communication. She edited *Represent*, Youth Communication's magazine by and for youth in foster care, for three years, and has written for a variety of publications. She has a BA in English from Tufts University and an MS in Journalism from Columbia University.

Acknowledgments

Special thanks to the members of the Andrus Family Fund's BET program for their generous support of this book.

Thanks also the Harry Berberian, Education Coordinator at the Graham Windham agency in New York City, for his valuable editorial feedback.

More Helpful Books
From Youth Communication

Do You Have What It Takes? A Comprehensive Guide to Success After Foster Care. In this survival manual, current and former foster teens show how they prepared not only for the practical challenges they've faced on the road to independence, but also the emotional ones. Worksheets and exercises help foster teens plan for their future. Activity pages at the end of each chapter help social workers, independent living instructors, and other leaders use the stories with individuals or in groups. (Youth Communication)

The Struggle to Be Strong: True Stories by Teens About Overcoming Tough Times. Foreword by Veronica Chambers. Help young people identify and build on their own strengths with 30 personal stories about resiliency. (Free Spirit)

Depression, Anger, Sadness: Teens Write About Facing Difficult Emotions. Give teens the confidence they need to seek help when they need it. These teens write candidly about difficult emotional problems—such as depression, cutting, and domestic violence—and how they have tried to help themselves. (Youth Communication)

What Staff Need to Know: Teens Write About What Works. How can foster parents, group home staff, caseworkers, social workers, and teachers best help teens? These stories show how communication can be improved on both sides, and provide insight into what kinds of approaches and styles work best. (Youth Communication)

Out of the Shadows: Teens Write About Surviving Sexual Abuse. Help teens feel less alone and more hopeful about overcoming the trauma of sexual abuse. This collection includes first-person accounts by male and female survivors grappling with fear, shame, and guilt. (Youth Communication)

Real Jobs, Real Stories. Help teens identify and strengthen the skills they need to succeed in the workplace, while building their literacy skills and motivation to read. (Youth Communication)

The Fury Inside: Teens Write About Anger. Help teens manage their anger. These writers show how they got better control of their emotions and sought the support of others. (Youth Communication)

Always on the Move: Teens Write About Changing Homes and Staff. Help teens feel less alone with these stories about how their peers have coped with the painful experience of frequent placement changes, and turnover among staff and social workers. (Youth Communication)

Two Moms in My Heart: Teens Write About the Adoption Option. Teens will appreciate these stories by peers who describe how complicated the adoption experience can be—even when it should give them a more stable home than foster care. (Youth Communication)

My Secret Addiction: Teens Write About Cutting. These true accounts of cutting, or self-mutilation, offer a window into the personal and family situations that lead to this secret habit, and show how teens can get the help they need. (Youth Communication)

Growing Up Together: Teens Write About Being Parents. Give teens a realistic view of the conflicts and burdens of parenthood with these stories from real teen parents. The stories also reveal how teens grew as individuals by struggling to become responsible parents. (Youth Communication)

To order these and other books, go to:
www.youthcomm.org
or call 212-279-0708 x115

9 781935 552468